REVISED EDITION

IN LINCOLN'S FOOTSTEPS

A Historical Guide to the Lincoln Sites in Illinois, Indiana, and Kentucky

By
Don Davenport

Trails Books
Black Earth, Wisconsin

First Edition
First Printing, February, 1991
Second Printing, March 1992
Second Edition
First Printing, February 2002

Library of Congress Control Number: 2001097358
ISBN: 1-931599-05-X

Editor: Jerry Minnich
Design: Kortney Kaiser
Cover Design: Kortney Kaiser
Photos: Don Davenport
Printer: McNaughton & Gunn

Printed in the United States of America
06 05 04 03 02 6 5 4 3 2

Trails Books, a division of Trails Media Group, Inc.
P.O. Box 317 • Black Earth, WI 53515
(800) 236-8088 • e-mail: books@wistrails.com
www.trailsbooks.com

For Mary Jo

CONTENTS

"With malice toward none; with charity for all; with firmness in the right, as God gives us to see the right, let us strive to finish the work we are in; to bind up the nation's wounds; to care for him who shall have borne the battle, and for his widow, and his orphan—to do all which may achieve and cherish a just and lasting peace, among ourselves and with all nations . . ."

A. Lincoln, March 4, 1865

Introduction

This is a travel guide, not a biography of Abraham Lincoln. The sketches of Lincoln's life and historical events are written as such—profiles that, I hope, make these places where Lincoln lived and worked, laughed and loved and wept, more interesting and meaningful to visit. The politics and issues of Lincoln's day—in particular the attitudes and practices concerning slavery—were highly complex and controversial, and are only outlined briefly. For those who wish to explore them further, a short reading list can be found at the back of this book.

Every attempt has been made to be historically accurate. I apologize for any errors that may come to light.

Illinois, Indiana, and Kentucky have approximately three thousand historical markers commemorating Abraham Lincoln or those associated with him. Some of the relationships are tenuous, at best. At the outset, the major criterion for sites to be included in this book was that they were to offer visitors a substantial experience. Some historically significant locales, offering little more than a sign, or a boulder and plaque, are not included. A few, if they are located close to major Lincoln sites, have been mentioned briefly. Fewer still—because they are works of art or are in some way unique—are included for their inherent qualities. Site selection was subjective.

The sites have been arranged in chronological order, in so far as practicable. In a few cases—namely the sections on the Eighth Judicial Circuit and Lincoln-Douglas Debates—this arrangement may not present the most efficient way of touring them.

With planning, it is possible to tour several Lincoln sites in a reasonably short time. A brief session with a road map will bring to light several easy weekend jaunts.

I grew up in Freeport, Illinois, where Abraham Lincoln and Stephen A. Douglas went at it hammer and tongs in the second of their great debates during the summer and autumn of 1858. That made visits to places where Lincoln lived or worked a special experience for me, and produced a wide range of emotions.

Listening to interpreters share their knowledge and feelings for the place and the man, interviewing Lincoln scholars, actors, and historians, witnessing ceremonies that commemorate his life more than 130 years after his death, intensified the experience. I hope to share some of that experience in the pages that follow.

Don Davenport
Monroe, Wisconsin
March 1, 2001

Acknowledgments

In retrospect, Miss Helen Graham, who taught fourth grade at Harlem School in Freeport, Illinois, planted the seeds for this book in 1944. She made sure her students understood that the Lincoln-Douglas debate held in Freeport was the important debate.

Special thanks go to Nicky Stratton, Executive Director of the Springfield, Illinois, Convention and Visitors Bureau, whose support and enthusiasm for this project has been immensely helpful. She, along with her staff, has been a wellspring of information and makes visits to Springfield a great pleasure.

Also in Springfield, many thanks go to Thomas F. Schwartz, Illinois State Historian; Norman Helmers, Superintendent of the Abraham Lincoln Home National Historic Site; Timothy Townsend, Lincoln Home Historian; and Timothy Good, Lincoln Home Park Ranger, who have been exceedingly gracious with their time and Lincoln expertise.

Thanks, too, to Vivah Harris, Executive Director of the Spencer County Visitors Bureau, in Santa Claus, Indiana, and to Melanie Maxwell, of Maxim Communications, Greensburg, Indiana, for their many contributions to this book.

A tip of the hat goes to Rick Rego, of Oshkosh, Wisconsin, for his many contributions to this and other projects over the years.

And special thanks go to Mary Jo Goecks, my wife and best friend, for her steadfast support through good times and bad.

To her, and all the others, I am extremely grateful.

Abraham Lincoln Chronology

May, 1782 Lincoln's grandparents, Abraham and Bersheba Lincoln, settle near Springfield, Kentucky.

June 12, 1806 Lincoln's parents, Thomas Lincoln and Nancy Hanks, are married near Springfield, Kentucky.

February 10, 1807 Nancy Hanks Lincoln gives birth to a daughter, named Sarah, in Elizabethtown, Kentucky.

February 12, 1809 Abraham Lincoln is born on Sinking Spring Farm near Hodgenville, Kentucky.

Spring, 1811 The Lincolns move to Knob Creek Farm near Hodgenville, Kentucky.

1812 Thomas Lincoln, Jr. is born at Knob Creek, but dies within a few days.

December, 1816 The Lincolns leave Knob Creek and settle at Little Pigeon Creek in Perry County, now Spencer County, Indiana.

October 5, 1818 Abraham Lincoln's mother, Nancy Hanks Lincoln, age thirty-five, dies of milk sick at Little Pigeon Creek.

December 2, 1819 Thomas Lincoln marries Sarah Bush Johnston, a widow with three children, in Elizabethtown, Kentucky.

January 20, 1828 Lincoln's sister, Sarah Lincoln Grigsby, dies in childbirth at age twenty-one.

April, 1828 Lincoln, age nineteen, and Allen Gentry pilot a flatboat to New Orleans.

March 1-15, 1830 The Lincolns leave Indiana and settle in Macon County, Illinois, near Decatur.

April, 1831 Thomas and Sarah Bush Lincoln leave Macon County and settle in Coles County, Illinois. Abraham Lincoln, John Hanks, and John Johnston pilot a flatboat to New Orleans for Denton Offutt.

July, 1831 Lincoln settles in New Salem, Illinois.

September, 1831 Lincoln, age 22, begins clerking in Denton Offutt's store at New Salem.

March 9, 1832 Lincoln becomes a candidate for the Illinois General Assembly.

April, 1832 The Black Hawk War breaks out and Illinois' governor calls for volunteers. Lincoln enlists in the local militia and serves for fifty-one days, but sees no action.

August, 1832 Lincoln is defeated in his bid for the Illinois General Assembly.

March 7, 1833 President Jackson appoints Lincoln postmaster at New Salem.

August 4, 1834 Lincoln, in his second try for public office, is elected to the Illinois General Assembly as a representative from Sangamon County.

August, 1836 Lincoln is re-elected to the Illinois General Assembly.

September 9, 1836 Lincoln receives his license to practice law.

February, 1837 Illinois General Assembly passes the act moving the state capital from Vandalia to Springfield. Lincoln and other members of the "Long Nine," a group of nine Whig party members elected from Sangamon County, all of whom are over six feet tall, are instrumental in getting the bill passed.

April 15, 1837 At age 28, Lincoln moves from New Salem to Springfield and becomes the law partner of John T. Stuart. He arranges to share a room with Joshua Speed, a Springfield store owner.

August 6, 1838 Lincoln is re-elected to a third term in the Illinois General Assembly, again as a Whig candidate.

September 23, 1839 Attorney Lincoln began traveling Illinois' Eighth Judicial Circuit. Save for two years when he serves in the United States House of Representatives, as part of the Thirtieth Congress, he continues to ride the circuit until elected to the Presidency.

1840 Lincoln and Mary Todd, who meet at a Springfield ball in 1839, begin courting.

AUGUST 3, 1840 Lincoln is re-elected to a fourth term in the Illinois General Assembly.

JANUARY 1, 1841 Lincoln and Mary break their engagement, most likely due to the disapproval of her sister and brother-in-law, Elizabeth and Ninian Edwards.

APRIL 14, 1841 Lincoln's law partnership with John T. Stuart ends. He soon becomes a law partner with Stephen T. Logan.

NOVEMBER 4, 1842 Lincoln and Mary Todd are married by the Reverend Charles Dressler. They move into the Globe Tavern in Springfield.

AUGUST 1, 1843 The Lincolns' first child, Robert Todd, is born at the Globe Tavern.

JANUARY 16, 1844 Lincoln buys the house at Eighth and Jackson Streets in Springfield.

DECEMBER, 1844 Lincoln and William H. Herndon become law partners. The partnership lasts until Lincoln's death.

MARCH 10, 1846 The Lincolns' second child is born and is named Edward Baker.

AUGUST 3, 1846 Lincoln is elected to the U.S. House of Representatives and serves one two-year term in office.

FEBRUARY 1, 1850 The Lincolns' second son, Edward Baker, dies after an illness of fifty-two days.

DECEMBER 21, 1850 The Lincolns' third son, William Wallace, is born.

JANUARY 17, 1851 Thomas Lincoln dies in Coles County, Illinois. Lincoln does not attend his father's funeral.

APRIL 4, 1853 The Lincolns' fourth son, Thomas (Tad), is born.

FEBRUARY 8, 1855 Lincoln is defeated in bid for U.S. Senate.

MAY, 1856 The Illinois Republican party is born at a convention in Bloomington. Lincoln gives the keynote address, not recorded, known as the "Lost Speech."

JUNE, 1856 Lincoln is nominated for Vice President at the Republican National Convention in Philadelphia. He receives 110 votes, but Ohio's William Dayton is nominated for Vice President.

MAY 7, 1858 Lincoln successfully defends Duff Armstrong in the famous Almanac Trial at Beardstown.

JUNE 16, 1858 Lincoln is the choice of Illinois Republicans for U.S. Senate. Responds with his famous "House Divided" speech.

AUGUST-OCTOBER, 1858 The Lincoln-Douglas debates are held at Ottawa, Freeport, Jonesboro, Charleston, Galesburg, Quincy, and Alton.

NOVEMBER 2, 1858 Lincoln loses the Senate race to Stephen A. Douglas.

MAY 10, 1860 Lincoln is nominated for President at the Illinois State Republican Convention in Decatur.

MAY 18, 1860 Lincoln is nominated for President on the third ballot by the Republican National Convention in Chicago.

NOVEMBER 6, 1860 Abraham Lincoln is elected the first Republican President of the United States.

DECEMBER 16, 1860 Ordinance of disunion is passed at Charleston, South Carolina. The Confederacy is formed.

DECEMBER 20, 1860 South Carolina secedes from the Union.

JANUARY 9, 1861 Mississippi secedes from the Union.

JANUARY 10, 1861 Florida secedes from the Union.

JANUARY 11, 1861 Alabama secedes from the Union.

JANUARY 19, 1861 Georgia secedes from the Union.

JANUARY 26, 1861 Louisiana secedes from the Union.

FEBRUARY 11, 1861 Lincoln delivers his "Farewell Address" in Springfield.

FEBRUARY 16, 1861 Jefferson Davis is sworn in as President of the Confederacy.

FEBRUARY 23, 1861 Texas secedes from the Union.

MARCH 4, 1861 Lincoln is inaugurated as the sixteenth President of the United States.

APRIL 12, 1861 First shots of the Civil War are fired at Fort Sumter, Charleston, South Carolina.

APRIL 17, 1861 Virginia secedes from the Union.

MAY 6, 1861 Arkansas secedes from the Union.

MAY 20, 1861 North Carolina secedes from the Union.

JUNE 8, 1861 Tennessee secedes from the Union.

FEBRUARY 20, 1862 William Wallace (Willie) Lincoln dies in Washington, D.C.

NOVEMBER 19, 1863 Lincoln delivers his famous Gettysburg Address at Gettysburg, Pennsylvania.

APRIL 9, 1865 General Robert E. Lee surrenders the Army of Northern Virginia to General Ulysses S. Grant at Appomattox, Virginia, ending the Civil War.

APRIL 14, 1865 Lincoln is shot by actor John Wilkes Booth in Ford's Theatre, Washington, D.C.

APRIL 15, 1865 Abraham Lincoln dies at 7:22 A.M. in the home of William Petersen.

APRIL 18, 1865 Lincoln's body lies in state in the East Room of the White House.

APRIL 19, 1865 Funeral services are conducted for Lincoln in the East Room of the White House.

APRIL 19-20, 1865 Lincoln's body lies in state in the Capitol Rotunda.

APRIL 21, 1865 Funeral train bearing the bodies of Abraham Lincoln and William Wallace Lincoln departs Washington. Arrives in Springfield May 3.

MAY 3-4, 1865 Lincoln's body lies in state at Old State Capitol.

MAY 4, 1865 Lincoln is buried in Oak Ridge Cemetery, Springfield.

Prologue

Abraham Lincoln stood tall even before he grew larger than life. Six feet four, with a size fourteen shoe, he walked with a stoop, usually with his hands clasped behind his back. The familiar top hat accentuated his height; clothes hung on him. His voice was thin and high pitched, growing shrill when he was excited, but it carried to the farthest corners of any crowd that gathered to hear him speak.

Lincoln spoke a frontier Indiana dialect, acquired during fourteen hard years in that state's southern wilds. He "sot" down, came "outen" the house, "heered" things, and "keered" for his family and friends. Although time and experience tempered the accent, he addressed the heads of meetings and conventions as "Mr. Cheermun" for all of his days. Yet he could be an eloquent speaker, especially so if he prepared well in advance, and some of his best speeches were his shortest.

He had a good sense of humor and was renowned as a storyteller; some of his stories were not for mixed company. But there was a dark side to him too, and he was often moody and withdrawn, prone to long spells of melancholy. Lincoln knew it, made occasional references to his moods in letters, and spoke of his moodiness as the "hypo."

Lincoln personified the American Dream before America had words for it—or perhaps he was its inadvertent father. Born in a Kentucky log cabin, with less than a year's education picked up "by littles," he grew up to become the President of the United States. From a log cabin to the White House. What would the politicians of today give for such a provenience?

He came to Illinois in 1830, drifted into New Salem and settled a year later. He knew hard work, had helped carve farms from wilderness, had split thousands of fence rails, had carried, lifted, and labored most of his young life. But he didn't much care for it and wanted to earn his living with his mind, not his muscles.

At twenty-three, Lincoln turned to politics. He ran for the Illinois legislature in 1832, lost the election, tried again two years later and won. He learned the law from books and was licensed to practice in 1836. Soon after, he left New Salem for Springfield.

He was a shrewd country lawyer and had three different partners in his lifetime. The last, William Herndon, stayed with him for twenty-one years. Lincoln rode the circuit, traveling Illinois' Eighth Judicial Circuit six months of the year, and stayed at it from 1839 until he was elected President. He defended big business, rapists, murderers, and slaveholders, handled divorces, tax cases, and property settlements, championed battered wives. His fees were lower than most—other lawyers gave him some grief about it—and he handled more than one case free of charge. He also sued clients who didn't pay.

In the courtroom, Lincoln had a way with juries. He spoke to them in their language, made his points in terms they understood. He often ambushed opposing lawyers who didn't know him well, played the country bumpkin, set them up, and swooped in for the kill. He argued two hundred cases before the Illinois Supreme Court and won most.

By all accounts, Lincoln and Herndon's office was a shambles—messy, cluttered, at times almost dysfunctional. Lincoln carried important papers around in his hat, put his partner's share of the proceeds in envelopes marked "Herndon's half," and kept an envelope for Herndon marked "If you can't find it anywhere else, look in here."

Lincoln's personal life was far from ideal. He buried his mother and sister in Indiana, buried one son in Illinois, another in Washington. He got on poorly with his father and was not especially close to his oldest son. But he revered his stepmother and adored his three youngest sons.

Women made Lincoln uncomfortable and his luck with them was not all that good. His one true love, if you believe some accounts, was Ann Rutledge, of New Salem, who died at age twenty-two. He had a short, unhappy romance with Mary Owens, then married sharp-tongued Mary Todd. She called him "Mr. Lincoln"—"Father" after their first-born arrived, and he called her "Mother." His friends and contemporaries called him "Lincoln," or "Mr. Lincoln." Few called him "Abe," at least to his face, for he disliked the name.

A shrewd and honest politician, Lincoln understood people and the system. He believed in the Republic and the Declaration of Independence and held what was considered a moderate stance on slavery, the burning issue of his time. He was an old line Whig—Kentuckian Henry Clay was his idol—and he became a Republican when the Whig party died in 1856.

The 1832 legislative race was the only popular election Lincoln lost, although he was twice rejected for Illinois' Senate seat by the state legislature. His arch political adversary was Democrat Stephen A. Douglas, and they battled each other across the width and breadth of Illinois for more than a quarter of a century. Their debates during the 1858 campaign for U.S. Senate made people outside of Illinois aware of Lincoln, just what he'd hoped when he challenged Douglas.

Lincoln was strictly a dark horse for the Republican Presidential nomination in 1860, although he admitted, "The taste is in my mouth a little." William H. Seward, of New York, was the top runner at the National Convention in Chicago, but Lincoln's supporters assembled a smooth-running machine that convinced the convention he could win. Lincoln was nominated on the third ballot, receiving 354 of 466 votes. He won the presidential election that November with only thirty-nine percent of the popular vote.

The first President to have been born in a log cabin, the first to have been born in a state other than the original thirteen states, and the first Republican President, Lincoln held office at a terrible time in the nation's history. By the day of his inauguration, on March 4, 1861, seven states had seceded from the Union and Jefferson Davis was President of the Confederacy. Six weeks later, the first shots were fired at Fort Sumter, and the nation was at war with itself. By June, another four states were gone from the Union. Three years of carnage and destruction followed, with Americans killing Americans on American soil.

It was foregone that Lincoln could not win the 1864 election. No President since Andrew Jackson had won reelection, and the war had ripped the nation asunder. There was talk of replacing him as the presidential nominee, but when the party met in Baltimore, in June, Lincoln gained the nomination.

Even Lincoln had doubts about reelection. In August, he wrote a memorandum and had his Cabinet sign it unread. It read:

"This morning, as for some days past, it seems exceedingly probable that this Administration will not be re-elected. Then it will be my duty to so co-operate with the President elect, as to save the Union between the election and the inauguration; as he will have secured his election on such ground that he cannot possibly save it afterwards."

But the Union was not ready to change horses in mid-stream and, with the Republicans running as the Union party, Lincoln carried twenty-two of the twenty-five states in the Union, losing only in Delaware, Kentucky, and New Jersey. He gave his Second Inaugural Address with its famous line "With malice toward none; with charity for all . . ." on March 4, 1865. Forty-two days later he was dead, killed by John Wilkes Booth's bullet. At the moment of his death, a tearful Edwin Stanton, the Secretary of War, murmured, "Now he belongs to the ages."

Indeed.

Kentucky

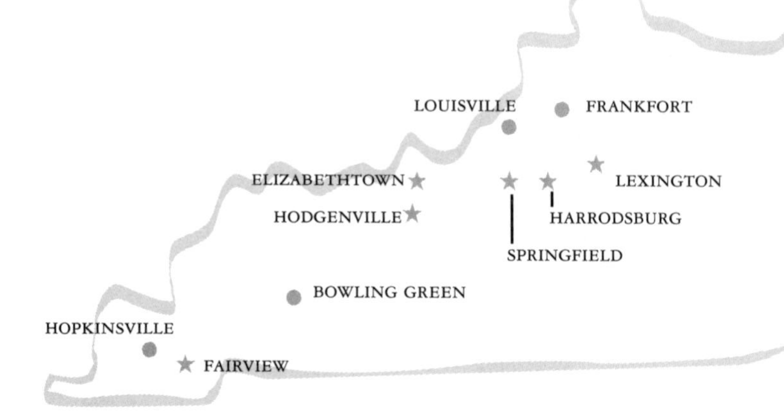

★ KEY LINCOLN CITIES

● KENTUCKY CITIES

Part I

The Kentucky *Years*

"It is a great piece of folly to attempt to make anything out of me or my early life. It can all be condensed into a single sentence, and that sentence you will find in Gray's Elegy, 'The short and simple annals of the poor.' That's my life, and that's all you or anyone else can make out of it."

A. Lincoln 1860

LINCOLN HOMESTEAD STATE PARK

Springfield, Kentucky

Francis Berry Home,
Lincoln Homestead State Park
Springfield, KY.

LOCATION: Five miles north of Springfield on Route 528; Washington County.

HOURS: Open daily 10-6, May through September; closed the rest of the year.

ADMISSION: Adults $1.50; ages 6-12, $1.

ACCESSIBILITY: Pathways are packed gravel, buildings have one or two steps.

INFORMATION: Lincoln Homestead State Park, 5079 Lincoln Park Road, Springfield, KY 40069; tel. 859-336-7461.

GETTING THERE: Springfield is 15 miles southeast of Bardstown, KY, on U.S. 150.

Set off in a corner of Lincoln Homestead State Park, this small historic site marks the beginning of our Lincoln trail. It was here that the Lincoln family first settled in Middle America and, more important, here that Abraham Lincoln's parents met and were married.

What Happened Here

In the central part of Washington County, a tributary of the Salt River called Beech Fork makes a horseshoe bend and carves out a region known as Beechland. In 1781 or '82, Abraham Lincoln's grandfather—Captain Abraham Lincoln—left Virginia and migrated here over Daniel Boone's Wilderness Road. The Lincolns settled a one hundred-acre tract of land purchased from Richard Berry, Sr. Lincoln and his wife, Bersheba, had five children—Mordecai, Josiah, Mary, Thomas, and Nancy. With his sons' help, Lincoln built a cabin near a small creek that became known as Lincoln's Run.

Captain Lincoln was the eldest son of John and Rebecca Flowers Morris Lincoln, and was born in Berks County, Pennsylvania, in 1744. As a young man he moved with his family to Virginia where he served in the Virginia Militia (hence the title, captain) and possibly the Revolutionary War. He married Bersheba Herring in 1770. They lived in the Shenandoah Valley until the lure of land holdings in the West drew them to Kentucky.

Still a Virginia county, Kentucky was then a wild, unsettled land, fraught with hardship and danger. In May of 1786, as Captain Lincoln was working with his sons in a field on the homestead, an Indian hiding in the woods shot and killed him. Terrified, eight-year-old Thomas huddled over his father's body while Josiah, thirteen, ran for help. Fifteen-year-old Mordecai ran to the family cabin for his father's gun. As the Indian crept toward the frightened Thomas, Mordecai returned, took careful aim, squeezed off a shot, and "brought him to the ground."

The fate of nations sometimes balances on such events, for Thomas Lincoln grew up to become Abraham Lincoln's father.

Today three log buildings mark the old Kentucky homestead. A replica of the frontier home where Bersheba Lincoln raised her five children, and where Thomas Lincoln lived for twenty-five years, rests on the same spot as the original. Built of logs more than one hundred years old, the cabin furnishings include several primitive pieces made by Thomas Lincoln, which are highlighted by a handsome corner cupboard. Tradition has it that Lincoln's grandmother buried her husband near the cabin; the location of the grave is unknown.

Nearby, down a winding path and across a small covered footbridge spanning Lincoln's Run, is a replica of a tiny blacksmith and carpenter shop much like the one in which Thomas Lincoln was to learn his trade. The tools of the trade—the forges, anvils, grindstones, lathes, hammers, and tongs—have changed surprisingly little in two centuries, and the shop looks much like those few working blacksmith shops that are occasionally found today.

Across the green from the Lincoln cabin is the original home of Francis Berry, brother of Richard Berry and an early Washington County settler. The home originally stood in the Beechland region, a mile away, and was moved here in 1941. One member of Berry's household was a young woman from Virginia named Nancy Hanks. Thomas Lincoln and Nancy Hanks took a shine to each other and it was in this two-story log home that Tom courted Nancy. Tradition holds that he proposed to her before the huge living room fireplace.

The house is furnished with early pioneer relics. A photocopy of the marriage bond between Thomas Lincoln and Nancy Hanks is displayed in the living room. It reads:

KNOW ALL MEN BY THESE PRESENTS THAT WE, THOMAS LINCOLN AND RICHARD BERRY, ARE HELD AND FIRMLY BOUND UNTO HIS EXCELLENCY, THE GOVERNOR OF KENTUCKY, IN THE JUST AND FULL SUM OF FIFTY POUNDS, CURRENT MONEY, TO THE PAYMENT OF WHICH, WELL AND TRULY TO BE MADE TO THE SAID GOVERNOR AND HIS SUCCESSORS, WE BIND OURSELVES, HEIRS, ETC., JOINTLY AND SEVERALLY, FIRMLY BY THESE PRESENTS, SEALED WITH OUR SEALS, AND DATED THIS 10TH DAY OF JUNE, 1806. THE CONDITION OF THE ABOVE OBLIGATION IS SUCH THAT, WHEREAS THERE IS A MARRIAGE SHORTLY INTENDED BETWEEN THE ABOVE BOUND THOMAS LINCOLN AND NANCY HANKS, FOR WHICH A LICENSE HAS BEEN ISSUED. NOW, IF THERE BE NO LAWFUL CAUSE TO OBSTRUCT THE SAID MARRIAGE, THEN THIS OBLIGATION TO BE VOID, ELSE TO REMAIN IN FULL FORCE AND VIRTUE IN LAW.

THOMAS LINCOLN. (SEAL)
RICHARD BERRY. (SEAL)
GARDIN WITNESS, JOHN H. PARROTT.

While such a bond seems strange today, it was in keeping with the Kentucky marriage laws of the day, which were based on an old English law dating from 1540.

Thomas Lincoln and Nancy Hanks were typical of their times on the early American frontier.

Thomas was born in Rockingham County, Virginia, in 1778 and was, as Abraham Lincoln later wrote, "even in childhood . . . a wandering laboring boy, and grew up literally without education." He was of average height, thick chested, with strong arms, a leathery complexion, and coarse black hair.

After his father's death, Thomas sometimes hired out to farmers in Washington County and learned to be a skillful carpenter. He could read a little, but "never did more in the way of writing than to bunglingly sign his own name," as his son recalled years later. In his middle teens, Thomas began to roam (a trait that stayed with him throughout his life), lived for a time with relatives in Tennessee, and eventually settled in Hardin County, Kentucky. In 1803 he bought a 288-acre farm on Mill Creek, about eight miles north of Elizabethtown, Kentucky, for 118 pounds cash. (Pounds and shillings were still used in Kentucky at the time.) His mother, his sister, and her husband left Washington County to join him there.

The life of Nancy Hanks is a genealogist's nightmare of myth, mystery, and legend. According to a notation Abraham Lincoln made in the family Bible, she was born in Virginia on February 5, 1784. When and how she came to Kentucky are unknown. Richard Berry, who co-signed the Lincoln-Hanks marriage bond, appears to have been her guardian. Yet she also had family in Kentucky. An aunt, also named Nancy Hanks, gave birth to an illegitimate son named Dennis Friend Hanks, in Hardin County in 1799. Thomas and Elizabeth Sparrow were also relatives, perhaps an aunt and uncle, and Dennis Hanks lived with them.

Nothing is known of Nancy Hanks' father. Lincoln himself seems to have believed his mother was born out of wedlock to a Lucy Hanks, who later married a man named Henry Sparrow.

There is even disagreement on what Nancy Hanks looked like—her height, build, the color of her eyes and hair. Acquaintances recalled her as intelligent, deeply religious, kindly, and affectionate.

William Herndon, Abraham Lincoln's law partner and a Lincoln biographer, wrote that Nancy Hanks had more education than her husband and taught him read and to write his name. But since she signed legal documents with her mark, this hardly seems likely. Nancy's mark was a shaky X which Thomas verified in equally shaky writing. It was usually written like this:

THOMAS LINCOLN
HER
NANCY X LINCOLN
MARK

Accounts written soon after Abraham Lincoln's death often described his mother as a saint and an angel. Perhaps Lincoln remembered her in that way. But in all probability, Nancy Hanks was an illiterate frontier woman who married a nearly illiterate frontier man and worked hard to raise a family under circumstances which were, at best, difficult.

Thomas Lincoln and Nancy Hanks were married at Richard Berry's Beechland home on June 12, 1806, the Reverend Jesse Head presiding. The bride was twenty-two years old, the groom twenty-eight.

Little else is known about the wedding. For a typical wedding celebration of the times, however, neighbors came from miles around and made a day of it. The wedding feast (perhaps prepared by Berry's slaves) would have offered venison, turkey, mutton—possibly bear—barbecued whole over a pit of coals and covered with green boughs to retain the juice. There would have been pies and home-baked bread, maple sugar for sweetening, and whiskey—certainly for the men, and not a few of the women, for liquor flowed freely on the early frontier. A neighbor might have brought a fiddle and played such pioneer favorites as "Turkey in the Straw," "Sugar in the Gourd," and "The Girl I Left Behind Me," while the celebrants danced late into the night. As the evening wound down, there would be coarse jokes about the wedding night.

After their marriage, Thomas and Nancy Lincoln moved to Elizabethtown. Bersheba Lincoln remained at Mill Creek until she died in 1836 at an old age.

Tours of the Lincoln buildings at Lincoln Homestead State Park are self-guided. Tickets are sold in a small gift shop near the Lincoln cabin, which features Kentucky handcrafts and souvenirs. A small fieldstone enclosure near the Berry House serves as a memorial to Nancy Hanks. While the site lacks the frontier feeling of other early Lincoln locales, the events that shaped the lives of the Lincolns who lived here had significance far beyond the death of an early Kentucky settler and the marriage of an illiterate frontier couple. But for Mordecai Lincoln's timely and accurate shot, the history of this nation after 1860 may well have been different.

Lincoln Homestead State Park: The 120-acre park has a regulation eighteen-hole golf course, picnic shelters, tables, grills, and a children's playground. Admission: Free. Additional information: Lincoln Homestead State Park, 5079 Lincoln Park Road, Springfield, KY 40069; tel. 859-336-7461.

Mordecai Lincoln Home: Located across the road from the park golf course is the home built by Abraham Lincoln's uncle in 1797. It is said to be the only remaining residence, still standing on its original site, known to have been owned and occupied by a member of the Lincoln family. However, the two-story log cabin built by Mordecai Lincoln was encased and enlarged by the Federal-style frame building visible today between the years 1810-1815, by the home's second owner, Wilfred Hayden. It can be viewed by driving by, but is not open for tours. Located four miles north of Springfield on Route 528.

Springfield, Kentucky (pop. 3,000)

A number of historic homes and buildings are found in and around Springfield; some are open to visitors. The Springfield Chamber of Commerce offers literature and directions to several historic buildings.

Washington County Courthouse: The courthouse houses a number of documents pertaining to Lincoln history and exhibits a copy of the Lincoln-Hanks marriage bond.

Completed in 1816, the picturesque courthouse is the oldest still in use in Kentucky. It stands at the corner of Main and Cross Streets and is open Monday-Friday 8:30-4:30, Saturday 9-noon; closed Sunday and holidays. Additional information: Washington County Courthouse, Main Street, Springfield, KY 40069; tel. 859-336-5410.

SORGHUM-TOBACCO FESTIVAL: The two-day festival held the first week in October features molasses-making demonstrations (molasses is made from the sorghum plant), an art and crafts show, and other events.

Nearby Accommodations:
Days Inn (62 rooms), 324 Lincoln Park Road, Springfield, KY 40069; tel. 800-544-8313 or 859-336-7550.

Maple Hill Manor Bed & Breakfast and Gift Shop, 2941 Perryville Road, Springfield, KY 40069, offers bed and breakfast accommodations in a thirteen-room mansion (c. 1851) that is listed on the National Register of Historic Places; tel. 800-886-7546 or 859-336-3075.
www.bbonline.com/ky/maplehill

Additional Information:
Springfield-Washington County Chamber of Commerce, 112 Cross Main Street, Springfield, KY 40069; tel. 859-336-3810.
www.ltadd.org/springfield

"I was born Feb. 12, 1809, in Hardin County, Kentucky."

A. Lincoln

ABRAHAM LINCOLN BIRTHPLACE NATIONAL HISTORIC SITE

Hodgenville, Kentucky

Lincoln birthplace memorial, Hodgenville, KY.

LOCATION: Three miles south of Hodgenville on U.S. 31E and Route 61; LaRue County (part of Hardin County until 1843).

HOURS: Open daily 8-6:45, Memorial Day through Labor Day; 8-4:45, rest of the year; closed New Year's Day, Thanksgiving Day, and Christmas Day.

ADMISSION: Free.

ACCESSIBILITY: Major park attractions, the picnic area, and restrooms are wheelchair accessible. A short boardwalk leads through the forest to the Memorial Building. Ask for information and assistance at the visitor center.

INFORMATION: Lincoln Birthplace National Historic Site, 2995 Lincoln Farm Road, Hodgenville, KY 42748; tel. 270-358-3137 or 270-358-3138. www.nps.gov/abli/

GETTING THERE: Hodgenville is nine miles south of Elizabethtown, KY, on Route 61.

If there is one spot in Middle America where Lincoln's memory is truly deified, it is at the birthplace. Here, where Nolin Creek winds through the hard Kentucky hills, Abraham Lincoln was born on a cold February morning, in a crude log cabin on a hill above a trickling spring.

What Happened Here

After their marriage, Thomas and Nancy Lincoln had moved to Elizabethtown where they lived in a house described by some as little more than a shed in one of the town's back alleys. On February 10, 1807, the couple's first child was born, a girl, whom they named Sarah. With dark hair and gray eyes, the baby resembled her father and as she grew older was remembered as having been short and stocky.

In "E-town," as it is known, Thomas earned a living as a common laborer, doing simple odd jobs, carpentry, and cabinet making. Always restless and ready to move on, in December of 1808 he bought a farm called Sinking Spring, paying $200 for 348 acres of stony land on Nolin Creek. Located fourteen miles southeast of Elizabethtown, the farm was named for a spring that flowed through a cavelike channel in a hill and dropped into a deep basin in the rock.

Sinking Spring Farm was not especially fertile. It stood on the edge of the Barrens, a great expanse of land made treeless by Indian fires set to create grazing land for game. Perhaps the Lincolns bought it because it was closer to Nancy's relatives and only three miles south of Robert Hodgen's mill (now present-day Hodgenville).

Sarah was less than two years old and Nancy was expecting another child when the Lincolns moved to Sinking Spring. Tradition says that Thomas Lincoln built a rude one-room cabin on the hill above the spring, although a dwelling may have existed here when he purchased the farm.

While the Kentucky winter deepened, Nancy's time drew near. On Sunday, February 12, 1809, as she lay near the fire on a bed of cornhusks and bear skins, Nancy Hanks Lincoln gave birth to a son. A local "granny woman," Aunt Peggy Walters, may have been present to assist with the delivery. The boy was named Abraham, after his grandfather.

(Seven months earlier, a child named Jefferson Davis was born in a Kentucky log cabin barely one hundred miles from Sinking Spring Farm. Abraham Lincoln and Jefferson Davis would cross paths many times in life, most notably when Lincoln was President of the United States and Davis was President of the Confederacy.)

During the two years they stayed at Sinking Spring Farm, the Lincolns lived the self-sufficient life of a Kentucky frontier farm family. Thomas continued to do a little cabinet-making and carpentry for neighborhood farmers, but he spent long hours behind a walking plow, trying to wrest a living from the red Kentucky clay, and tramping the woods with his rifle in search of game to feed his family. Nancy cared for her children and cooked simple meals—pork, corn, bread—in a Dutch oven and long-handled frying pan. By the spring of 1811, Thomas was ready to move again. The Lincolns left Sinking Spring for a farm on Knob Creek, ten miles to the east, where the soil was richer.

The birthplace cabin's historical value was recognized as soon as Abraham Lincoln became President. In 1861 Dr. George Rodman purchased the Lincoln farm and moved the remains of a log cabin—traditionally thought to be Lincoln's birthplace—to his own neighboring farm. It stood there for thirty-four years, until 1895, when New York businessman A. W. Dennett purchased the cabin and returned it to the Lincoln farm. Soon after it was dismantled and became a meandering exhibit, displayed at the Nashville Centennial in 1897, in New York's Central Park, and at the 1901 Buffalo Exposition. The cabin then disappeared for a time and was eventually found in storage in Long Island, New York.

In 1904 several famous Americans, among them author Mark Twain, publisher Robert Collier, politician William Jennings Bryan, and labor leader Samuel Gompers, formed the Lincoln Farm Association to preserve the birthplace and establish an Abraham Lincoln memorial. The association acquired the farm in 1905 and the cabin in 1906, and raised over $350,000 from more than 100,000 Americans for a shrine in which to house it.

Architect John Russell Pope was commissioned to design the memorial for which President Theodore Roosevelt laid the cornerstone in 1909. Two years later, President William Howard Taft dedicated the grandiose, neo-classical, marble and granite temple. The 116-acre site became a national park in 1916. It was designated the Abraham Lincoln Birthplace National Historic Site in 1959 and is today operated by the National Park Service.

A short film, "Lincoln—the Kentucky Years," which tells the story of Lincoln's early life, is shown in the visitor center auditorium on the hour and half-hour, and there are exhibits of tools and early nineteenth-century utensils representative of the era. The exhibit highlight is the Lincoln family Bible—"The Holy Bible Containing Old and New Testaments With Arguments Prefixed to the Different Books and Moral and Theological Observations Illustrating Each Chapter Composed by the Reverend Mr. Osterwald, Professor of Divinity." Within its covers is a page containing Thomas Lincoln's shaky signature and Nancy Lincoln's mark.

The visitor center also features an information desk and small bookshop with a good selection of publications related to Lincoln and the National Parks.

A short walk from the visitor center is the Doric-columned shrine that houses a very old log cabin. Each of fifty-six steps leading to the memorial represents a year in Lincoln's life. A small marker at the foot of the steps reads: "Abraham Lincoln was born in a small cabin overlooking the Sinking Spring. While lacking absolute proof, all traditions and available documentation support the belief that this cabin has been reconstructed with some of the original logs on or very near the birth site."

Above the six granite columns at the memorial entrance are carved these words from President Lincoln's Second Inaugural Address:

WITH MALICE TOWARD NONE,
WITH CHARITY FOR ALL

Chiseled into the marble beside the massive double bronze doors at the entrance is the inscription:

HERE OVER THE LOG CABIN WHERE
ABRAHAM LINCOLN WAS BORN, DESTINED TO
PRESERVE THE UNION AND FREE THE SLAVE,
A GRATEFUL PEOPLE HAVE DEDICATED THIS
MEMORIAL TO UNITY, PEACE, AND
BROTHERHOOD AMONG THE STATES

Bronze tablets at the entrance, rear, and inside the memorial are inscribed with portions of Lincoln's most memorable speeches. Sixteen ceiling rosettes symbolize him as the sixteenth President of the United States.

The memorial stands in stark contrast to its contents. The timeworn cabin it enshrines is shockingly small, about sixteen by eighteen feet. Its oak and chestnut logs—143 in all—are chinked with clay. Rough wooden shingles cover the roof. There is a stone fireplace, one door and one window, without glass, once covered with greased paper or thin animal skin. A small, box-like stick-and-clay chimney is tacked on one end. The floor is dirt. There are no furnishings.

As much as one wants to believe, it is now generally accepted that this is not the cabin in which Abraham Lincoln was born, although some of the logs are believed to be of the period.

Regardless, all the grade school lessons about Lincoln's humble beginnings are driven home. The cabin is a powerful image to accompany the restrained references Lincoln made in later life to his early "years of stinted living."

Below the hill, the Sinking Spring still sparkles and gurgles, just as when Thomas, Nancy, Sarah, and Abraham Lincoln drank its waters. Recessed in a small, cool cavern, it is reached by a short flight of cobblestone steps.

Years after the Lincolns left Sinking Spring, a small oak sapling along the farm's south edge became known as the Boundary Oak. The tree grew to a height of nearly one hundred feet and lived until the nation's bicentennial in 1976—the last living vestige of the Kentucky farm where Abraham Lincoln was born.

Elsewhere in the park are marked nature trails, restrooms, and a picnic area; camping is not allowed.

The park hosts several programs during the year—National Park Day is observed in August and Martin Luther King, Jr.'s birthday is celebrated in January. A Lincoln's Birthday wreath-laying ceremony is held each February 12.

Nearby Accommodations:
See Hodgenville, Kentucky.

"My earliest recollection is of the Knob Creek place."

A. Lincoln

Abraham Lincoln's Boyhood Home
Hodgenville, Kentucky

Lincoln boyhood home, Knob Creek Farm, Hodgenville, KY.

Location: Seven miles northeast of Hodgenville on U.S. 31; LaRue County.

Hours: Open daily 9-5, April 1-October 31, (open until 6 P.M. Memorial Day-Labor Day); closed the rest of the year.

Admission: Adults $1; ages 6-12, 50¢; age 5 and under, free.

Accessibility: Gravel pathway, one step to historic cabin. No wheelchair accessible restrooms.

Information: Knob Creek Farm, U.S. 31E, Hodgenville, KY 42748; tel. 502-549-3741.

The Knob Creek Farm is rich in the history and tradition of Lincoln's early Kentucky years. A reconstructed log cabin stands on the site of the Lincoln homestead; there is a gift shop offering books, specialty items, and displays of nineteenth-century tools and artifacts.

What Happened Here

The Lincolns moved to Knob Creek in the spring of 1811, when Abraham was two. Here he grew to boyhood and was introduced to the physical labor that would mark the early decades of his life—carrying water, gathering wood for the fire, and working in the fields.

The main road between Louisville and Nashville ran close to the homestead cabin and here young Lincoln had his first views of the outside world. There were covered wagons filled with settlers passing by, and itinerant peddlers carrying their wares on their backs. On occasion he saw gangs of slaves in the possession of overseers or slave traders.

In later years, Lincoln recalled many memories of his days at Knob Creek: a stone house he had passed on the way to Hodgen's mill, the creek where he fished, the hills where he gathered berries. He had vivid memories of planting pumpkin seeds in alternate hills and rows while the oldsters planted corn, only to have a big rain wash the seeds away. Once, while crossing swollen Knob Creek on a log, Lincoln fell into the water and boyhood chum Austin Gollaher fished him out with a sycamore branch.

Nancy Lincoln gave birth to her third child at Knob Creek in 1812. The boy was named Thomas, after his father, but died within a few days of birth. Thomas Lincoln made a pine coffin and buried his son near the cabin, on a knob called Mulldraugh's Hill.

On the rare occasions when they could be spared from their chores, Sarah and Abraham walked two miles to school. In the dirt-floored log school they sat on benches with no backrests and learned the alphabet and elements of reading, writing, and arithmetic. It was a "blab school" where the students learned their lessons by repeating them aloud, over and over. Their teachers were Zachariah Riney and Caleb Hazel, a neighbor whose father was the local tavernkeeper. Lincoln recalled little about the school in later life, except that he spent perhaps three months there.

Three years after he moved to Knob Creek, Thomas Lincoln fell victim to Kentucky's chaotic land laws. In 1814 he sold the Mill Creek Farm for one hundred pounds, eighteen pounds less than he had paid for it. The loss came from a flaw in the title; the farm contained thirty-eight acres less than he assumed. Then he became involved in litigation over the Sinking Spring farm. The title to the Knob Creek Farm came under dispute and a suit was filed to dispossess him. Disheartened, Thomas decided to move to Indiana where the land had been marked by government survey.

It has been suggested that Thomas Lincoln left Kentucky because he was against slavery. It is possible. At Knob Creek, Thomas was a member of the Little Mount Separate Baptist Church, which had broken with the regular church over the slavery issue. Hardin County in 1811 had just over one thousand slaves and about 1,600 white males over age sixteen. As a common laborer, Thomas had to compete for wages against men who earned no wages.

In later years, Lincoln said his father decided to leave Kentucky "partly on account of slavery; but chiefly on account of the difficulty in land titles." For whatever reason, Thomas Lincoln decided to pull up stakes and leave Kentucky. Tradition says that he made a preliminary trip to look over the new land. In December of 1816, the Lincolns set out for Indiana with all their personal possessions. Abraham was seven years old.

The Knob Creek Farm is listed on the National Register of Historic Places. The original Lincoln cabin was torn down in 1870 and replaced in 1931 with a cabin reconstructed with logs from the home of Austin Gollaher, the boy who pulled Lincoln from Knob Creek. The pioneer cabin is furnished with an eclectic collection of artifacts, some from the Lincoln period. There are picnic facilities on the grounds.

On a knoll across the highway from the cabin is the unkept cemetery where Thomas Lincoln, Jr. was buried, however the stone that marked the baby's grave has been removed.

Two miles northeast of Knob Creek, near the town of Athertonville, a historical marker notes the location of the school that Abraham and Sarah Lincoln attended. Austin Gollaher's grave is indicated by a historical marker at the Pleasant Grove Baptist Church, just off U.S. 31.

Nearby Accommodations:
See Hodgenville, Kentucky.

Hodgenville, Kentucky (pop. 3,449)

The Hodgen's mill the Lincolns knew became Hodgenville in 1818. The symbol of the community's Lincoln legacy is a large bronze statue of Lincoln in the public square. The work of sculptor Adolph A. Weinman, the statue depicts Lincoln seated, his head bowed, in a pensive mood. The six-foot high figure was dedicated in 1909 during the centennial anniversary of Lincoln's birth. (A replica of the statue is located on the campus of the University of Wisconsin at Madison.)

Lincoln statue by Adolph Weinman, Hodgenville, KY.

LINCOLN MUSEUM: Located on Hodgenville's public square, the museum features Lincoln-era artifacts, a permanent collection of paintings and art, galleries for traveling exhibits, and a video presentation of Lincoln's Kentucky years. Dioramas and life-size wax figures create twelve scenes from Lincoln's life, including the Lincoln-Douglas debates, the Knob Creek Farm, the Presidential box in Ford's Theatre, Washington, D.C. (where

Lincoln was assassinated), and the Gettysburg Address. The museum shop offers books, gifts, and specialty items. The museum is open year round, Monday-Saturday 8:30-4:30, Sunday 12:30-4:30; closed holidays. Lower level exhibits, including the Lincoln dioramas and restrooms, are wheelchair accessible. Admission: Adults $3; age 60 and up, $2.50; ages 5-12, $1.50; under 5, free. Additional information: Lincoln Museum, 66 Lincoln Square, Hodgenville, KY 42748; tel. 270-358-3163.

Lincoln Days: Hodgenville celebrates Lincoln Days on the second weekend in October with rail-splitting contests, parades, Lincoln lookalikes, craft demonstrations, Little Abe and Sarah contests, and other events.

Nearby Accommodations:
Cruise Inn Motel (10 rooms), 2768 Lincoln Farm Road (Route 31 E.), Hodgenville, KY 42748; tel. 270-358-9998.

Old Gaite Farm Bed and Breakfast offers accommodations in a 1917 Victorian farm house: 7281 Bardstown Road, Hodgenville, KY 42748 (mail to P.O. Box 291, New Haven, KY 40051); tel. 502-549-7348.
www.bbonline.com/ky/oldegait/index.html

Joel Ray's Family Restaurant, 2579 Lincoln Farm Road, tel. 270-358-3545.

Stewarts Restaurant, 330 S. Lincoln Boulevard, tel. 270-358-9344.

Additional Information:
LaRue County Chamber of Commerce, 58 Lincoln Square, P.O. Box 176, Hodgenville, KY 42748; tel. 270-358-3411.
www.laruecountychamber.org/

Related Lincoln Sites in Kentucky

Elizabethtown (pop. 20,000)

Lincoln Heritage House: This double log home was the dwelling of Elizabethtown pioneer Hardin Thomas and his family. The first cabin was built in 1789. The second, and larger of the two, was built with the help of family friend Thomas Lincoln in about 1805. Lincoln also crafted the stairways, fireplace mantles, and most of the homes' "woodwork. Located two miles northwest on U.S. 31W, then east at Freeman Lake Park. Open Tuesday-Sunday 10-5, June through September; closed the rest of the year. Admission: free. Additional information: tel. 800-437-0092 or 270-765-2175.

Sarah Bush Johnston Lincoln Memorial: The fourteen by fourteen-foot memorial cabin was built in 1992, Kentucky's Bicentennial year, from hand-hewn logs that were 122 years old. It is a close replica of the Elizabethtown cabin in which the widow Sarah Bush Johnston was living with her daughters, Elizabeth and Matilda, and son, John, when the widower Thomas Lincoln returned to Elizabethtown in the autumn of 1819 to propose marriage. Thomas Lincoln and Sarah Bush Johnston were married in E-town on December 2, 1819, in an old log house that stood at the present address of 117 North Main Street. A copy of their marriage bond may be found at the local library.

Immediately after the wedding, Sarah and her children left Elizabethtown, traveling with Thomas by team and wagon to the Lincoln cabin in the wilds of Southern Indiana. Sarah never returned to Kentucky again.

The memorial cabin is located in Freeman Lake Park, near the Lincoln Heritage House. Open daily on summer afternoons, other times by appointment. Admission: free. Additional information: tel. 800-437-0092 or 270-765-2175. A stone marker on the grounds of the Hardin County Courthouse in Elizabethtown commemorates Thomas and Nancy Hanks Lincoln's first home in the community.

Nearby Accommodations:
Comfort Inn Atrium Gardens (133 rooms), I-65 Exit 94, 1043 Executive Drive, Elizabethtown, KY 42701; tel. 800-682-5285 or 270-769-3030.

Red Roof Inn (96 rooms), I-65 Exit 94, 2009 North Mulberry Street, Elizabethtown, KY 42701; tel. 270-765-4166.

Additional Information:
Elizabethtown Tourism and Convention Bureau, 1030 North Mulberry Street, Elizabethtown, KY 42701; tel. 800-437-0092 or 270-765-2175. www.ltadd.org/etowntourism/

Fairview (pop. 200)

Jefferson Davis Monument State Historic Site: The shrine marks the site where the President of the Confederacy was born on June 3, 1806, and features a 351-foot obelisk, one of the largest monuments in the U.S. An elevator takes visitors to an observation room high atop the monument. A celebration marking Davis' birthday is held the first weekend in June. The site is located nine miles east of Hopkinsville on U.S. 68 and is open daily 9-5, May through October; closed the rest of the year. Admission: Adults $2; ages 6-12, 50¢. Additional information: tel. 270-886-1765. www.state.ky.us/agencies/parks/jefdav2.htm

Harrodsburg (pop. 8,000)

Old Fort Harrod State Park: The site commemorates the first permanent English settlement west of the Alleghenies (1774). Among the park's many historic buildings is the double log cabin of Richard Berry, believed to be the cabin in which Thomas and Nancy Hanks Lincoln were wed. The cabin is housed in a church-like structure known as the Lincoln Marriage Temple. Located in the heart of Harrodsburg, the park is open daily 9-5:30, mid-March through October, daily

8:30-5 in November; closed the rest of the year. Admission: Adults $3.50; ages 6-12, $2. Additional information: tel. 859-734-3314. www.state.ky.us/agencies/parks/ftharrd2.htm

Lexington (pop. 236,000)

Mary Todd Lincoln House: The girlhood home of Abraham Lincoln's wife, the 1803 Georgian-style house has period furnishings and numerous artifacts of the Lincoln-Todd families. Located at 578 W. Main Street, the home is open Monday-Saturday 10-4, April 1 to December 15; closed the rest of the year. Guided tours are given continuously throughout the day. Admission: Adults $7; ages 6-12, $6. Additional information: tel. 859-233-9999.

Lexington Cemetery: The family of Mrs. Abraham Lincoln is buried here, as are Henry Clay and numerous other famous Kentuckians. Located at 833 W. Main Street, the cemetery is open daily 8-5.

Additional Information:
Lexington Convention and Visitors Bureau
301 E. Vine Street, Lexington, KY 40507-1513
tel. 800-845-3959 or 859-233-7299. www.visitlex.com/

Additional Information about Kentucky:
The Kentucky Department of Travel
500 Mero Street #2200, Frankfort, KY 40601
tel. 502-564-4930. www.kytourism.com/

Indiana

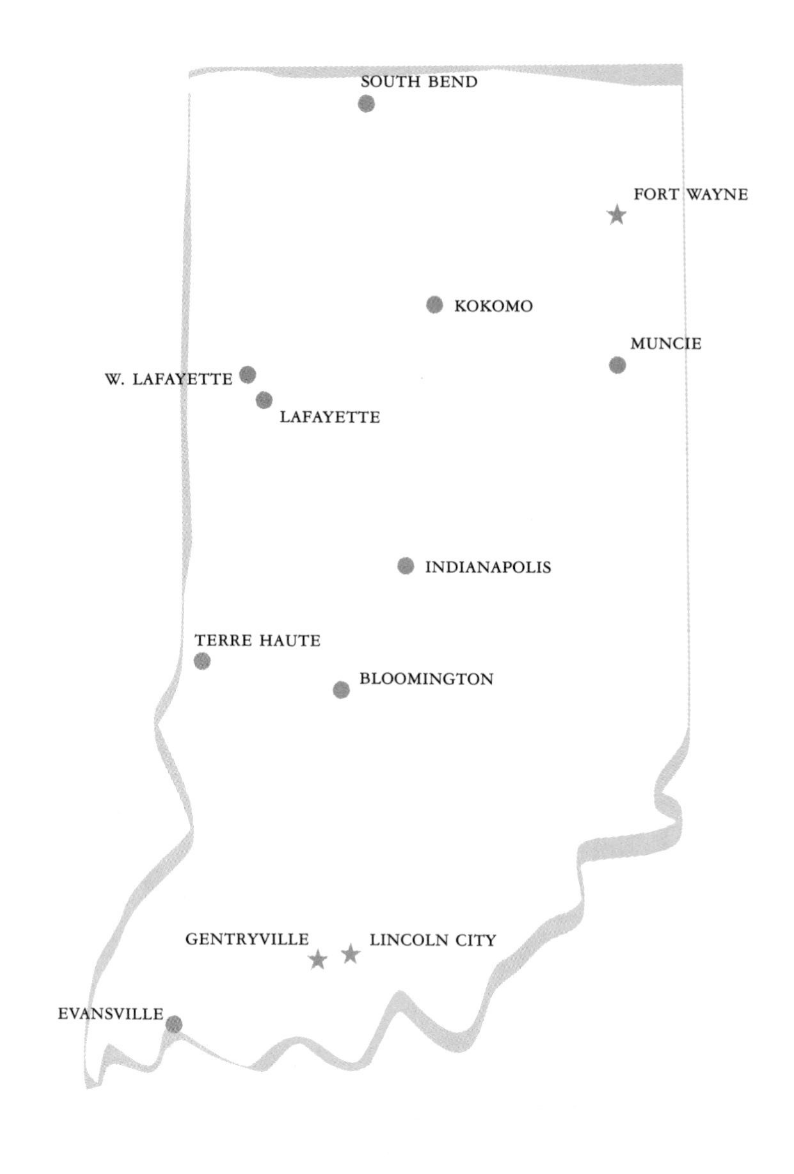

★ KEY LINCOLN CITIES

● INDIANA CITIES

Part 2

The Indiana *Wilderness*

"It was a wild region, with many bears and other wild animals still in the woods."

A. Lincoln, 1860

"Here I grew up."

A. Lincoln

LINCOLN BOYHOOD NATIONAL MEMORIAL

Lincoln City, Indiana

Living History Farm, Lincoln Boyhood National Memorial, Lincoln City, IN.

LOCATION: Two miles east of Gentryville, IN, on Route 162; Spencer County.

HOURS: Open daily, summer 8-6, winter 8-5; closed Thanksgiving, Christmas, and New Year's Day. Living History Farm open daily mid-April through October.

ADMISSION: Adults (age 17 and up) $2 per person, maximum charge $4 per family.

ACCESSIBILITY: Wheelchair accessible, including restrooms and historic cabin site; services also available to visually impaired and hearing-impaired visitors. Ask for information and assistance at visitors center.

INFORMATION: Lincoln Boyhood National Memorial, P.O. Box 1816, Lincoln City, IN 47552-1816; tel. 812-937-4541. www.nps.gov/libo/index.htm

GETTING THERE: Take exit 57 off I-64, travel south five miles on U.S. 231, turn east on Route 162, and follow the signs to Lincoln Parks.

So strongly tied to Illinois is Abraham Lincoln's image that the fourteen years he spent in the forests of southern Indiana are often overlooked. They were among the most difficult years of Lincoln's life—"pretty pinching times," as he later put it—and he buried both his mother and sister in the Indiana soil.

Lincoln's time on the Ohio River frontier is commemorated at the National Park Service's Lincoln Boyhood National Memorial. Off the beaten path, the memorial features a large and attractive visitors center, a small museum, and a "hands on" Living History Farm on the Lincoln homestead, where visitors are encouraged to handle most furnishings, tools, equipment, clothing, and similar articles.

Living History Farm, Lincoln Boyhood National Memorial, Lincoln City, IN.

WHAT HAPPENED HERE

The Lincolns reached the Ohio River at a point opposite Troy, Indiana, and, after crossing the river on a rude ferry, started northward through a forest undergrowth so dense that Thomas Lincoln had to go ahead and hack a trail. Sixteen miles north of the Ohio, Thomas chose a homesite, on a knoll a mile from Little Pigeon Creek.

It was December when the family arrived in Indiana. Thomas quickly threw up a "half-faced camp" to protect his family from the damp and cold. A brush and log lean-to, the shelter was closed on only three sides, with the open side protected by a fire kept blazing twenty-four hours a day. The nearest water was a mile away. Panthers and wildcats screamed in the forest and wolves howled at night.

Thomas filled their meager larder with what the land had to offer—raccoons, squirrels, deer, and bear from the forest; wild turkey, quail, and grouse from the underbrush; geese and ducks from the marshes. The family existed almost entirely on wild game until spring. Lincoln remembered that first winter in Indiana as one of the bleakest times in his life.

By February, when Abraham turned eight, Thomas had a new one-room log cabin ready. Barely eighteen feet square, it had a packed dirt floor, a stick-and-mud chimney, and a stone fireplace used for both cooking and heating. Abraham slept in the cabin's unheated loft, which he reached by climbing pegs driven into the cabin wall.

The spring the Lincolns drew water from on the Little Pigeon Creek Farm, Lincoln Boyhood National Memorial, Lincoln City, IN. It was an open spring in Lincoln's time.

That spring Lincoln's father handed him an ax and set him to work—clearing fields, chopping wood, splitting fence rails. For an 1860 campaign biography, written in the third person, Lincoln wrote, "Abraham, though very young, was large of his age, and had an ax put into his hands at once; and from that till within his twentythird year, he was almost constantly handling that most useful instrument—less, of course, in plowing and harvesting seasons." Life in the "unbroken wilderness," he later said, was a fight "with the trees and logs and grubs."

In the autumn of 1817, Nancy Lincoln's relatives, Thomas and Elizabeth Sparrow, and her cousin, Dennis Hanks, joined the family at Little Pigeon Creek and spent the winter in the half-faced camp the Lincolns had abandoned. Although Dennis Hanks was ten years older than Abraham, the two became close friends. In his later years, Hanks offered many insights into Lincoln's early years, although his tales did not always have the solid ring of truth.

Tragedy—the first of many in Abraham Lincoln's life—struck the Lincoln household in the autumn of 1818, as an epidemic of the "milk sick" swept southwestern Indiana. It is now believed drinking milk from cows poisoned by the white snakeroot plant caused the illness. But all the pioneers knew about milk sick was that it struck quickly and usually brought death. In September, Thomas and Betsy Sparrow fell ill and died within a few days. Thomas Lincoln built two rough coffins and buried his neighbors on a nearby knoll.

Then Nancy Lincoln became ill. She died on October 5, at the age of thirty-five. Once again a sorrowful Thomas Lincoln built a coffin. Some accounts say that nine-year-old Abraham whittled the pegs that held the pine boards together. As the family made preparations for burial, the body lay in the same room where they ate and slept. They buried her on the knoll beside the Sparrows, on a brilliant autumn day when the Indiana hills were ablaze with color. No minister spoke over the grave; Nancy Hanks Lincoln's funeral was as homemade as her coffin.

Dennis Hanks moved in with the Lincolns and, while twelve-year-old Sarah took over the cabin chores and kept house for the three men, Thomas, Abraham, and Hanks hacked away at the forest and tended their meager crops. It was a black, dismal time for the Lincoln family, the worst of many lean years of poverty, hard times, and isolation. Of their Indiana years Dennis Hanks later said, "We lived the same as Indians, 'ceptin' we took an interest in politics and religion."

Nancy Hanks Lincoln's grave,
Lincoln Boyhood National Memorial,
Lincoln City, IN.

In late 1819, Thomas returned briefly to Elizabethtown, Kentucky, and proposed to Sarah Bush Johnston, a widow he had known for a decade. There were apparently few formalities. Sally, as the widow Johnston was known, is said to have replied, "I've got a few little debts," and Thomas took her list and paid them. They were married on December 2. Thomas piled Sally, her household goods, and children—Sarah Elizabeth (thirteen), Matilda (ten), and John D. Johnston (nine)—into a borrowed wagon and they set out for Indiana.

In 1865 Sally recalled Indiana as "wild and desolate . . .", the Lincoln cabin as "good . . . tolerably comfortable." The Lincoln children, she remembered, had to be dressed up to look "more human." Of Abraham she said, "He was the best boy I ever saw."

Bronzed sill logs and hearth stones of a very old cabin on or near the site of the Lincoln cabin at Little Pigeon Creek. Traditionally thought to be the Lincoln cabin. Lincoln Boyhood National Memorial, Lincoln City, IN.

Eight people now lived in the tiny cabin, but the Lincolns' fortunes were much improved. Sally was a kind stepmother who raised Abraham and Sarah as her own. Through love and hard work, she made the rough frontier cabin a home. At her insistence, Thomas put a floor in the cabin, built some decent beds and chairs, and made other improvements.

Though illiterate herself, Sally saw to it that Abraham got what little education the Indiana frontier had to offer. Schools operated infrequently—opening whenever a teacher arrived in the region and closing when the teacher left. Between his eleventh and fifteenth years, Lincoln spent time at "blab" schools run by Andrew Crawford, James Swaney, and Azel Dorsey, attending brief sessions between the autumn harvest and the spring plowing. Dorsey was well trained, and under his direction Lincoln probably received his best education. Years later Dorsey could still remember Abraham as "marked for the diligence and eagerness with which he pursued his studies, (he) came to the log-cabin schoolhouse arrayed in buckskin clothes, a raccoonskin cap and provided with an old arithmetic." Dorsey moved to Schuyler County, Illinois, in 1828, where he taught school. Coincidentally, he lived out his years not far from Lincoln's Springfield home. Dorsey died in 1858 and is buried on a farm near the hamlet of Huntsville, Illinois, sixty-five miles northwest of Springfield.

Abraham could outspell all the other pupils in school and did all of the writing for his family and much of it for his neighbors.

At home he ciphered on boards, then shaved them clean with a hunting knife to start the next lesson. In a homemade copy book he wrote a boyish poem:

ABRAHAM LINCOLN
HIS HAND AND PEN
HE WILL BE GOOD BUT
GOD KNOWS WHEN

Young Lincoln was a voracious reader and, while books were scarce on the frontier, he read and reread those he could find—*Weem's Life of Washington, Robinson Crusoe, Pilgrim's Progress, Aesop's Fables, Grimshaw's History of the United States.* Tradition says rain coming through cracks in the cabin ruined a copy of the Life of Washington he had borrowed from Josiah Crawford, and Lincoln pulled fodder on Crawford's farm for three days to pay for it.

In all, Abraham Lincoln had less than a year of formal education, picked up "by littles." "There was absolutely nothing to excite ambition for education," Lincoln said of his schooling in Indiana. Still, he could read, write, and cipher to the rule of three by the time his family left the state.

By the 1820s, a rough settlement had grown up at Little Pigeon Creek, with some thirty families homesteading in a four by six-mile region. But conditions remained primitive. Sanitation was little understood and people went for seasons without baths. Farming required backbreaking labor and the superstitious pioneers planted and harvested by the phases of the moon. Women and children went barefoot most of the time. Epidemics wiped out entire families. Almost everyone drank heavily. Nearly all frontier social events revolved around work—cabin raisings, corn-shuckings, quilting bees.

As the widespread settlement grew, the Baptists chose Thomas Lincoln to build the log Pigeon Creek Baptist Church, which he and Sally joined. James Gentry opened a store in his farmhouse, a few miles from the Lincoln cabin. Gentry's place soon became the local trading center and grew into the village of Gentryville. Lincoln spent much of his spare time there, listening and swapping yarns and stories with the neighborhood farmers. He could be a jovial storyteller and companion, but he could also be moody, serious, and withdrawn.

Thomas Lincoln occasionally hired his son out to other homesteaders. While Abraham disliked farm work, he could be counted on to deliver a day's work for a day's wages, although farmers sometimes found him reading a book at the end of a plow furrow while allowing the horse to "breathe." "My father taught me to work," Lincoln once said, "but he didn't teach me to like it." He turned whatever he made, usually about twenty-five cents a day, over to his father, who legally commanded his wages until Abraham became of age.

Work-hardened, Lincoln grew tall and angular, strong in his arms, legs, and chest, like his father. As a teenager he could grasp an ax by the handle and hold it at arm's length with little effort. His skill with an ax became legendary. "If you heard him felling trees in a clearing," said a neighbor, "you would say there were three men at work, the way the trees fell."

At age seventeen Abraham left home for about nine months and went to work for James Taylor, who operated a ferry on Anderson Creek, where it entered the Ohio near Troy. He was paid thirty-seven cents a day for what he described long after as, "the roughest work a young man could be made to do." Lincoln built a small scow in his spare time and once ferried two travelers out to a packet boat on the Ohio. After he hoisted their luggage aboard the packet, each threw a silver half-dollar into the bottom of his little boat. It was an event he remembered long after.

Lincoln's sister, Sarah, grew up and married Aaron Grigsby, a neighborhood farmer. But just two years later, on January 20, 1828, Sarah died in childbirth at the age of twenty-one. She was buried, her stillborn child in her arms, in the cemetery beside the church her father had built.

That spring Lincoln contracted with James Gentry to take a boatload of farm produce down to New Orleans. In April he and Allen Gentry—one of James's sons—shoved off from Rockport, twenty miles from Little Pigeon Creek, and guided their flatboat on the 1,200-mile journey down the Ohio and Mississippi.

New Orleans was the first city that Lincoln had seen. Over a thousand flatboats—piled high with produce from Missouri, Illinois, Indiana, and Ohio—were tied up at the wharves when Lincoln and Gentry arrived. They sold their boat and produce, then explored the city. They watched the square-rigged sailing ships leave for ports around the world, took in the French Quarter with its picturesque homes and ladies of the night, saw the slave markets where black men, women, and children were auctioned off like so much produce. The trip, and the city, made a lasting impression on the nineteen-year-old Lincoln.

Grave of Sarah Lincoln Grigsby and her husband, Aaron Grigsby, Little Pigeon Creek Baptist Church Cemetery, Lincoln State Park, Lincoln City, IN.

They made part of the journey back to Indiana by steamboat, their fare paid by James Gentry, and reached Little Pigeon Creek in July. Lincoln earned twenty-four dollars for his three-month labors; he dutifully handed the money over to his father.

But there was now an estrangement between father and son. Some blamed it on Thomas, saying he thought Abraham was ruining himself with education and that he beat his son for reading books. Others said Abraham was openly hostile, with a great deal of it aimed at his father's intellectual limitations. For whatever reasons, Thomas and Abraham drew far apart in Indiana and seldom saw each other after the early 1830s.

Young Lincoln now began spending time at the log courthouses at Rockport and Boonville, watching the lawyers argue cases and listening to speculation on how various trials might turn out. The law intrigued him and he borrowed and read the Revised Statutes of Indiana. He also studied the Declaration of Independence and the Constitution, and closely watched how lawyers used them in the courtroom.

Like most places he lived, Indiana did not meet Thomas Lincoln's expectations. After fourteen years he was no better off than when he arrived. The milk sick was a constant threat. When John Hanks, a cousin of Nancy's who had lived on and off with the Lincolns in Little Pigeon Creek, sent word from Illinois that the land there was fertile and there was no milk sick, Thomas once again caught "moving fever." In February, 1830, he and Sally sold the Little Pigeon Creek farm for $125.

By now the Lincoln clan had grown considerably. In 1821 Dennis Hanks had married Sally's daughter, Sarah Elizabeth (fifteen years old at the time), and the union had quickly produced four children. Sally's other daughter, Matilda, was married to a man named Squire Hall and they had one child. Counting Sally's son, John Johnston, and the three Lincolns, the extended family now totaled thirteen.

On March 1, 1830, they piled their belongings into three wagons and set out for Illinois. Abraham was twenty-one, legally free of his father and entitled to keep his wages. But he chose to go along, perhaps hoping, like the elder Lincoln, that Illinois would provide a brighter future.

Abraham Lincoln returned to the Little Pigeon Creek region only once, in 1844, when as a successful lawyer and politician he campaigned in Indiana for Henry Clay. The visit evoked such strong feelings that Lincoln later wrote poetry about it. Yet he was never nostalgic for the hard years in Indiana, and he allowed his mother's grave to go unmarked for all of his years.

Lincoln's true feelings for Nancy Hanks Lincoln were as shadowy as her origins. He devoted only three lines to her and the Hanks family in an 1860 campaign biography and almost never spoke of her. William Herndon, Lincoln's third law partner and biographer, wrote that Lincoln once said to him, "God bless my mother; all that I am or ever hope to be I owe to her." But some historians believe Lincoln was speaking of his stepmother, of whom he said "she proved a good and kind mother." And he always referred to her as "Mother" in his letters.

It was well after Lincoln's death before the importance of his Indiana years were fully recognized. Nancy Hanks Lincoln's weed-choked grave went unmarked until 1878, when South

Bend industrialist P. E. Studebaker had a stone placed there. A small county park created near the pioneer cemetery around the turn of the century was a popular picnic spot for many years. Lincoln State Park and the adjoining Nancy Hanks Lincoln State Memorial were built at Little Pigeon Creek in the 1930s. The memorial to Lincoln's mother, acquired by the National Park Service in 1962, has since become the Lincoln Boyhood National Memorial.

The memorial visitor center has a museum, two memorial halls, and a bookshop with a good selection of publications related to Lincoln and the National Parks. The building exterior features five large sculpted limestone panels by Indiana artist E. H. Daniels depicting important events in Lincoln's life. Interior hallway galleries offer changing exhibits on Lincoln and his years in Indiana. The exhibit includes many photos, paintings, and sculptures of Lincoln, including a life mask of Lincoln's hands and face by Chicago sculptor Leonard Volk, and a bust of Lincoln by the same E. H. Daniels who created the building's exterior panels.

Within the museum are period tools and artifacts, and small dioramas depicting several scenes from Lincoln's life, including Nancy Lincoln's funeral. No photos of Lincoln's mother exist, but a painting based on contemporary description shows her as young, attractive, and saintly. The museum highlight is a life-size cutaway of a one-room log cabin, which includes a corner cabinet built by Thomas Lincoln and the original hearthstones from the Lincoln's Pigeon Creek cabin. The Nancy Hanks Lincoln Hall, in one wing of the memorial, holds a tiny U.S. post office, which keeps the Lincoln City, Indiana, postmark alive. Another wing, called Abraham Lincoln Hall, houses a beautiful limestone-walled chapel.

"Here I Grew Up," a twenty-four-minute film about Lincoln's Indiana years, both deifies Lincoln and glamorizes the frontier life (as do similar films at Kentucky and Illinois sites), but offers interesting insights into the Little Pigeon Creek settlement.

Nancy Hanks Lincoln's grave lies on a knoll rising above a park-like mall, an easy, 250-yard walk from the visitor center. Here, in a small cemetery where other early pioneers lie at rest, is an unpretentious marker that reads:

NANCY HANKS LINCOLN
Mother of President
LINCOLN
Died
Oct. 5 A.D. 1818
Aged 35 Years
Erected by a friend of her martyred son
1879

The Lincoln cabin site memorial and Living History Farm are a quarter-mile north of the cemetery and can be reached by auto from the visitor center, by a direct foot trail from the cemetery, or by the half-mile Trail of Twelve Stones. Both trails cross the Lincoln Trace, the route the Lincolns followed to their Little Pigeon Creek homestead from the Ohio.

Indiana panel by E. H. Daniels, Lincoln Boyhood National Memorial, Lincoln City, IN.

The Trail of Twelve Stones features historic stones from places that were important in Lincoln's life, including a monument that once marked the site of the Spencer County cabin and stones from Lincoln's birthplace, Hodgenville, Kentucky; the Jones store, Gentryville, Indiana; the Western Sun newspaper building, Vincennes, Indiana; the Lincoln-Berry Store, New Salem, Illinois; Mary Todd Lincoln's girlhood home, Lexington, Kentucky; the White House, Washington, D.C.; President Lincoln's summer cottage, Washington, D.C.; the Civil War battlefield at Gettysburg; the Old Capitol Building, Washington, D.C.; the Petersen House, Washington, D.C.; and Lincoln's Tomb in Springfield, Illinois.

Lincoln Boyhood National Memorial, Lincoln City, IN.

The memorial's Living History Farm depicts a pioneer homestead much like the Lincolns might have known. There are rough-hewn log buildings, livestock, rail fences, and fields planted with the crops grown on this very land in Lincoln's time—corn, oats, cotton, flax, wheat, squash, pumpkins, and sunflowers.

While not original to the site, the homestead farm cabin is from the Lincoln period (circa 1820), moved here from a nearby location and reconstructed from parts of several period cabins. It stands on, or very near, the location of the original Lincoln home. The mud-chinked walls and plank floor are whitewashed, as Sally Lincoln dictated. The cabin has primitive period furnishings—a rough-hewn table, chairs, a dough box, early lanterns, and crockery. Pegs driven into the wall lead to an overhead loft. Park interpreters dressed in 1820s-style clothing cook meals in the fireplace, spin flax and wool, chop wood, tend livestock, plant and harvest farm crops. Visitors are invited to examine and touch many of the items in the cabin and on the farm.

Close by is a curious and strangely moving Lincoln memorial—bronzed sill logs and hearthstones from an old, old cabin, unearthed in 1934 when the Nancy Hanks Lincoln Memorial was begun. The sill and hearth mark "the traditional site of a log cabin home built by Thomas Lincoln and his son, Abraham."

Were they true remnants of the Lincoln cabin? Perhaps, perhaps not. But as much as any of the dozens of Lincoln memorials scattered throughout the Midwest, these bronzed artifacts deep in the Indiana forest graphically symbolize the difficult early years of this nation's sixteenth president.

Portion of original foundation, Little Pigeon Creek Baptist Church, Lincoln State Park, Lincoln City, IN.

Lincoln State Park: Located on Highway 162 across from the Lincoln Boyhood National Memorial, the 1,747-acre park's attractions include the Little Pigeon Creek Baptist Church and the cemetery where Abraham Lincoln's sister, Sarah, is buried (her grave marker is easy to find). A small portion of the church foundation is original. The church is still used for services and weddings, and visitors are welcome. Park recreational facilities include 85-acre Lake Lincoln, a lakeside shelter house, boat rental building, nature center, cabins, picnic areas, shelters and trails, Class A and primitive camp sites. Lincoln State Park is also the home of "Young Abe Lincoln" outdoor drama. The park is open year-round. Admission: Indiana residents, $2 per car, out-of-state residents, $5 per car. Additional information: Lincoln State Park, P.O. Box 216, Lincoln City, IN 47552; tel. 812-937-4710.

Young Abe Lincoln: This musical drama on Lincoln's life is presented in a roofed outdoor amphitheater on the very land where Lincoln and his family toiled during their Indiana years. The drama is presented at 7:30 P.M. from mid-June through mid-August; other musicals are included on the playbill. Additional information: Young Abe Lincoln, University of Southern Indiana, 8600 University Boulevard, Evansville, IN 47712; tel. 800-264-4223.
www.lincolnamphitheatre.com/index.htm

Gentryville, Indiana (pop. 300)

William Jones State Historic Site, Gentryville, IN.

WILLIAM JONES STATE HISTORIC SITE: The site showcases the restored home of Colonel William Jones, a merchant, farmer, politician, and soldier who built the Federal-style brick house in 1834.

According to tradition, Abraham Lincoln, whose boyhood home lies a few miles down the road, performed odd jobs for the Jones' before the Lincolns left the area in 1830. Lincoln stayed in the house in the fall of 1844 while campaigning for Henry Clay. When in his sixties, Jones joined the Union Army and had reached the rank of lieutenant colonel in the 53rd Regiment of Indiana Volunteers when he was killed in the Battle of Atlanta on July 22, 1864.

The house is a fine example of Federal style architecture and contains a second floor observatory. A corner cupboard in the kitchen is attributed to Thomas Lincoln. The site is located just west of US 231 on Boone Street in Gentryville, and is open 9-5 Wednesday-Saturday, 1-5 Sunday, mid-March to mid-December, closed Thanksgiving and Easter; admission free. Additional information: R.R. 1 Box 60D, Gentryville, IN 47537; tel. 812-937-2802. www.state.in.us/ism/sites/jones/

Nearby Accommodations:

Baymont Inn and Suites (75 rooms), Exit 57, I-64/US 231, 20857 N. US 231, Dale, IN 47523; tel. 800-301-0200 or 812-937-7000.

Motel 6 (62 rooms), Exit 57, I-64/US 231, 20840 N. US 231, Dale, IN 47523; tel. 812-937-2294.

Denny's Restaurant, Exit, I-64/US 231, Dale; tel. 812-937-4439.

Wendall's Café, 6 W. Metcalf, Dale; tel. 812-937-4253.

Buffalo Run (specializing in buffalo and ostrich), Hwy 162, Lincoln City, IN. tel. 812-937-2799.

Additional Information:
Spencer County Visitors Bureau, P.O. Box 202, Santa Claus, Indiana 47579; tel. 888-444-9252.
www.legendaryplaces.org/index.html

Learning More About Lincoln

The Lincoln Museum, Fort Wayne, Indiana

Although, as far as is known, Abraham Lincoln never visited Fort Wayne, the city's Lincoln Museum is the world's largest museum dedicated to interpreting and preserving the history and legacy of Abraham Lincoln.

Under the general heading of Abraham Lincoln and the American Experiment, Lincoln's life and times are explored in galleries titled Lincoln's America, Prairie Politician to President, Civil War, Ford's Theatre and Beyond, The Lincoln Family Album, Remembering Lincoln, and the A. Lincoln Gallery. Visitors can attend a rousing 1850s political meeting, see a life-size model of Lincoln guiding a flatboat down the Mississippi River, read original documents used to buy and sell slaves, see Lincoln's own photos of his family and much more. Original Lincoln artifacts, three dimensional multimedia presentations, interactive computer activities, and touchable reproductions, along with lectures and special events give additional scope to the exhibits.

The museum library holds nearly 18,000 published volumes and thousands of manuscripts, including more than 300 original

Lincoln documents. There's a museum shop offering some 1,600 Lincoln items, including a wide variety of books.

The museum is open Tuesday-Saturday from 10-5, Sunday 1-5, (library and archives open by appointment Tuesday-Friday); museum closed Monday and New Year's Day, Easter, Memorial Day, July 4, Labor Day, Thanksgiving, and Christmas. Admission: Adults, $2.99; age 60 and up, and ages 5-12, 1.99; under age 5 and museum members, free. Additional information: The Lincoln Museum, 500 East Berry Street, Fort Wayne, IN 46802; tel. 219/455-3864. www.thelincolnmuseum.org

Additional Information About Fort Wayne:
Fort Wayne/Allen County Convention and Visitors Bureau, 1021 South Calhoun Street, Fort Wayne, Indiana 46802; tel. 800-767-7752. www.fwcvb.org/

Additional Information About Indiana:
Indiana Tourism Development Division, Indiana Department of Commerce, One N. Capitol, Suite 700, Indianapolis, IN 46204-2288; tel. 888-ENJOY-IN. www.enjoyindiana.com/

ILLINOIS

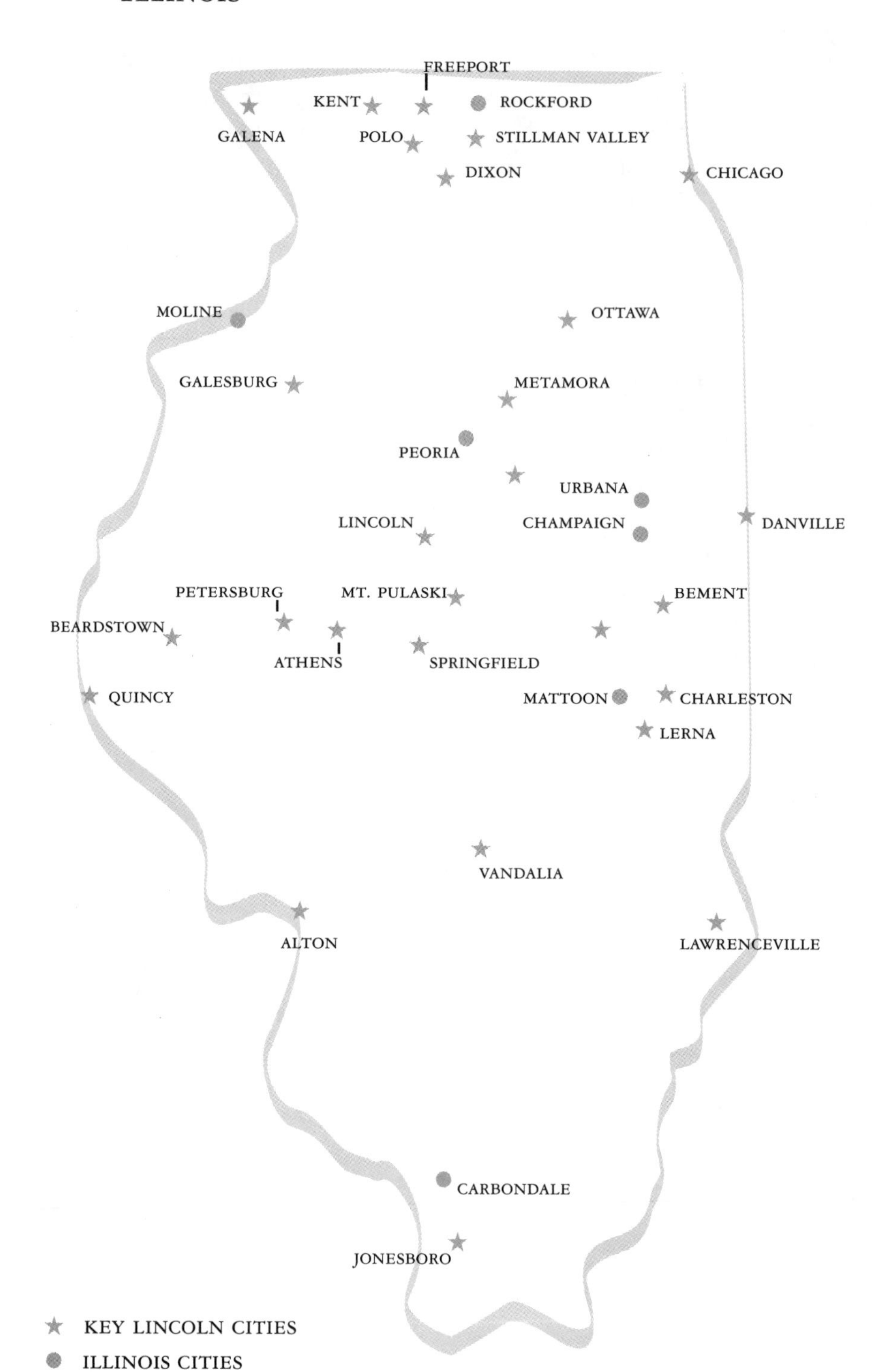

FREEPORT
KENT
ROCKFORD
GALENA
POLO
STILLMAN VALLEY
DIXON
CHICAGO
MOLINE
OTTAWA
GALESBURG
METAMORA
PEORIA
URBANA
LINCOLN
CHAMPAIGN
DANVILLE
PETERSBURG
MT. PULASKI
BEMENT
BEARDSTOWN
ATHENS
SPRINGFIELD
QUINCY
MATTOON
CHARLESTON
LERNA
VANDALIA
ALTON
LAWRENCEVILLE
CARBONDALE
JONESBORO
KEY LINCOLN CITIES
ILLINOIS CITIES

Part 3

Illinois
Land of Lincoln

"Fellow citizens, I presume you all know who I am. I am humble Abraham Lincoln. I have been solicited by my friends to become a candidate for the Legislature. My politics are short and sweet, like the old woman's dance. I am in favor of the national bank; I am in favor of the internal improvements system and a high protective tariff. These are my sentiments and political principles. If elected, I shall be thankful; if not, it will be all the same."

A. Lincoln - Pappsville, Illinois, 1832

First Home in Illinois
★*1830-1831*

Lincoln Trail Homestead State Park

Decatur, Illinois

Lincoln Trail State Memorial, marking the spot where the Lincoln family first entered Illinois.

Location: Ten miles west of Decatur on U.S. 36 to Lincoln Trail Memorial Parkway, then south four miles; Macon County.

Hours: Open daily dawn-dusk.

Admission: Free.

Accessibility: Wheelchair accessible with assistance.

Information: Lincoln Trail Homestead State Park, 705 Spliter Park Drive, Mt. Zion, IL 62549; tel. 217-864-3121.

Getting There: Decatur is 40 miles east of Springfield, 50 miles southwest of Champaign via I-72.

Although Macon County and Decatur are rich in Lincoln history, only historical markers indicate most events that took place here. There is a large boulder and bronze plaque marking the approximate site of the Lincoln homestead cabin.

WHAT HAPPENED HERE

The Lincoln party crossed the Wabash River at Vincennes, Indiana, and entered Illinois in Lawrence County, near present-day Lawrenceville, traveling primitive roads that were flooded over long stretches and covered with a thin skin of ice.

In 1860, Lincoln wrote of those first hours in Illinois:

". . . When I came to the water I put a favorite first dog I had along into the wagon and got in myself and whipped up my oxen and started into the water to pick my way across as well as I could—after breaking the ice and wading about 1/4 of a mile, my little dog jumped out of the wagon and the ice being thin he broke through and was struggling for life. I could not bear to lose my dog and I jumped out of the wagon, and waded waist deep in the ice and water, got hold of him and helped him out and saved him."

After a two-week journey of more than two hundred miles from Little Pigeon Creek, the Lincolns spent their last night on the trail, March 14, 1830, camped in a clearing in Decatur—then a hamlet of less than a dozen log cabins in a grove of oak trees. The next day they journeyed to the north bank of the Sangamon River, ten miles southwest of Decatur, and settled on land that Lincoln's cousin, John Hanks, had picked out for them.

The men raised a cabin with logs Hanks had previously cut, cleared and fenced some fifteen acres of land, and planted crops. In the summer, Abraham and John Hanks split several thousand rails for neighboring farmers. Many of the rails became political symbols or were sold as souvenirs three decades later.

That autumn most of the party fell ill with fever and ague, a common illness on the Illinois prairie at the time. Thomas Lincoln became so discouraged and disappointed with Illinois that he decided to return to Indiana the following spring.

The brutal winter of 1830-31 was known as the winter of the "big snows" in eastern Illinois. A raging blizzard struck in December and lasted for days. Freezing rain followed, then more snow and more rain. The temperature hovered at twelve degrees below zero for days on end. Livestock stranded in the fields perished, or were devoured by wolves. Whipped by bitter winds, snow drifted six feet high, marooning settlers in their cabins. Many froze to death for lack of wood to burn, or starved for lack of food. When the spring thaw came, floods ravaged the land.

In spring, 1831, Thomas and Sally Lincoln, along with most of the family, started back for Indiana. But Abraham did not go with them and he would never again live with his parents or extended family. In February, John Hanks had been hired by a frontier speculator named Denton Offutt to take a flatboat of produce to New Orleans. Hanks included Lincoln and his stepbrother, John Johnston, in the venture. And so as the Hankses, Halls, and elder Lincolns struck out on a journey that would lead them to settle in Coles County, Illinois, Abraham, Hanks, and Johnston bought a large canoe and paddled down the Sangamon River to Springfield, where they had arranged to meet Offutt.

While Abraham may not have realized it at the time, the event was a turning point in his life. The Lincoln legend in Illinois was about to begin.

"Lincoln's First Political Speech," by Tony Vestuto, Lincoln Square, Decatur, IL.

Decatur, Illinois (pop. 85,300)

The clearing where the Lincoln party camped in 1830 is now Lincoln Square, in downtown Decatur. It also marks the site of Lincoln's first political speech. In 1830, while working in a field near the little settlement, Lincoln heard a commotion in the public square and arrived at the scene in time to hear part of a speech against the Whig party. When the speaker finished, Lincoln is said to have mounted a stump and spoke in defense of the Whig candidate. A bronze statue commemorating the event, "Lincoln's First Political Speech," by Tony Vestuto, depicts a barefoot Lincoln with one foot on a stump and is located on the northeast corner of Lincoln Square. "Lincoln the Lawyer," an eight-foot statue by the sculptor Boris Lovet-Lorski, stands in the 200 block of E. Wood Street at the north entrance to the Macon County Building. "Lincoln at Twenty-one," a statue of a seated Lincoln with ax in hand, by sculptor Fred M. Torrey, is on the campus of Millikin University at Schilling Hall, on W. Main Street.

Lincoln argued many cases in Decatur as a circuit-riding attorney on the Eighth Judicial Circuit, which included Macon County. A log replica of the first Macon County Courthouse, where Lincoln practiced law, is located in the Macon County Museum Complex.

The Illinois Republican Convention, meeting in Decatur in May of 1860, unanimously endorsed Lincoln as a favorite son candidate for the Presidency. A Republican lawyer from Decatur, Richard J. Ogelsby, later governor of Illinois, arranged for John Hanks to bring to Decatur some of the rails Hanks had split with Lincoln thirty years before. At the convention, Ogelsby announced that an "old Democrat" wished to make a contribution. At that, Hanks came down the aisle with a friend, carrying a banner suspended between two rails which read:

ABRAHAM LINCOLN
THE RAIL CANDIDATE FOR PRESIDENT IN 1860
TWO RAILS FROM A LOT OF 3,000 MADE IN
1830 BY JOHN HANKS AND ABE LINCOLN—
WHOSE FATHER WAS THE FIRST PIONEER
OF MACON COUNTY

While Thomas Lincoln was not the first settler in Macon County, Lincoln's image as the "Rail Splitter" was made. And Hanks became so famous that he sold rails from the Macon County farm all over the country for one dollar per rail.

Hanks attended Lincoln's funeral in Springfield in 1865 and shortly thereafter capitalized on his early association with the slain President by displaying relics associated with Lincoln. Along with Dennis Hanks (also Lincoln's cousin) and another man, John Hanks purchased the Lincoln cabin in Macon County and exhibited it at a fair in Chicago in June of 1865. The Hankses then displayed the cabin at the Boston Common later that summer and sold souvenir canes made from Lincoln rails. After the cabin was displayed in P. T. Barnum's Museum in New York (the Barnum of "there's a sucker born every minute" fame), it disappeared from history. John Hanks died in Decatur in 1889, at the age of eighty-seven, and is buried in Boiling Springs Cemetery. Take Route 121 north to Riedel Avenue, turn left on Riedel, travel two blocks, then turn right on Tropicana; signs also point out the cemetery.

Other Decatur Attractions:

Macon County Historical Society Museum: The Prairie Years and the Victorian Era in Central Illinois come to life in the museum's indoor exhibits. In addition to the courthouse where Lincoln practiced law in 1830, the Prairie Village on the museum grounds is also home to a log house, a one-room school, a circa-1880 railroad depot, a smithy and a print shop. Located five miles east of downtown Decatur at 5580 North Fork Road, the museum is open year-round Tuesday through Sunday from 1-4. Admission: Free, donation suggested. Additional information: tel. 217-422-4919. www.fgi.net/~mchs/

Scovill Zoo: The 10-acre zoo features animals from around the world, living as they would in the wild, an oriental garden, picnic areas, and a train ride around the grounds. Located at 71 S. Country Club Road, the zoo is open Monday-Friday 10-4, Saturday-Sunday 10-6:30, mid-April to mid-October with extended evening hours June through August. Admission: $2.75 adults; $1 ages 3-11. Additional information: tel. 217-421-7435. www.decatur-parks.org/html/zoo.html

Nearby Accommodations:
Best Western Shelton Motor Inn (150 rooms)
450 E. Pershing Road, Decatur, IL 62526; tel. 217-877-7255.

Baymont Inn & Suites (106 rooms). I-72 and US 51 North
5100 Hickory Point Frontage Road, Decatur, IL 62526
tel. 217-875-5800.

The Blue Mill, 1099 W. Wood Street at Oakland Avenue
tel. 217-423-7717.

Jimmy Ryan's, 101 S. Main Street, tel. 217-422-4700.

Additional Information:
Decatur Area Convention and Visitors Bureau
202 E. North Street, Decatur, IL 62523;
tel. 800-331-4479 or 217-423-7000.
www.decaturcvb.com/

"I am not reading, I am studying the law."

A. Lincoln 1834

LINCOLN'S NEW SALEM STATE HISTORIC SITE

Petersburg, Illinois

LOCATION: Two miles south of Petersburg, 20 miles north of Springfield on Route 97; Menard County.

HOURS: Open daily 9-5, March-October, 8-4, November-February; closed New Year's Day, Martin Luther King, Jr. Birthday, Washington's Birthday (observed), Veterans Day, Thanksgiving, and Christmas.

ADMISSION: Suggested donation, fee for theater performances.

ACCESSIBILITY: Restrooms and museum wheelchair accessible; most village streets are hard surfaced. Assistance is available.

INFORMATION: Site Superintendent, Lincoln's New Salem State Historic Site, R.R.1, P.O. Box 244A, Petersburg, IL 62675; tel. 217/632-4000. www.lincolnsnewsalem.com/

GETTING THERE: Exit I-55 at Springfield, then travel north 20 miles on Route 97.

Set on a bluff overlooking the Sangamon River, this reconstructed village that was Lincoln's home from 1831 to 1837 is a Currier and Ives print come to life. Log homes and cabins line the dusty streets, gardens and crops are planted as they were in the 1830s, oxen and horses roam fields behind split-rail fences, wood smoke scents the prairie air.

Located in New Salem State Park, the village is both charming and historically significant, providing a vivid picture of nineteenth-century life on the Illinois prairie. It is easy to imagine Lincoln the storyteller regaling villagers with earthy tales before the fireplace at the Rutledge Tavern, or Lincoln the postmaster ambling down the street with the day's mail tucked inside his hat.

What Happened Here

After traveling the flood-swollen Sangamon from Decatur to near Springfield, Lincoln, John Hanks, and John Johnston walked five miles into the town and found Denton Offutt drinking at the Buckhorn Tavern. The promised flatboat for the trip to New Orleans had not been purchased, so Offutt hired the trio to build one for wages of twelve dollars a month. He sent them to government land on the Sangamon above Springfield, where they cut logs, had them sawed into planks at a nearby mill, and hammered together a crude eighty by eighteen-foot boat.

Top: Henry Onstot Cooper Shop, Lincoln's New Salem State Historic Site, Petersburg, IL.

Bottom: Rutledge Tavern, Lincoln's New Salem State Historic Site.

Offutt joined the party in mid-April and, with a cargo of barreled pork, corn, and live hogs, they cast off for New Orleans. A few miles down river they came to a dam across the Sangamon at the village of New Salem. When they tried to force their clumsy craft across, it caught halfway over and began to take on water. A crowd of excited onlookers called out advice while Lincoln had the cargo redistributed to balance the boat. He then went ashore, borrowed an auger at Henry Onstot's cooper shop, and bored a hole in the boat to let the water out. With the hole plugged, the flatboat was poled over the dam and the crew climbed the bluff to visit the village. It was Lincoln's first sight of the place that would change his life.

New Salem was then two years old, founded in 1829 by James Rutledge and John Camron, who built the dam on the Sangamon and constructed a lumber and gristmill. As the mill began to draw trade, Samuel Hill and John McNeil opened a store on the bluff above. In October of 1829, Rutledge and Camron hired a surveyor to plan and lay out a town they called New Salem. They sold the first lot on December 24, for twelve dollars and fifty cents. A post office was established in Hill and McNeil's store on Christmas Day with Samuel Hill as postmaster. Mail came to the village once a week from Springfield, twenty miles away.

Settlement in Illinois moved from south to north and, when Lincoln first saw New Salem, few villages of any size existed to the north. Peoria was only a fledgling town and Chicago had a population of perhaps one hundred people, living in a few log cabins huddled around Fort Dearborn. The lead mines at Galena were just beginning to draw settlers. Dixon's Ferry, where the trail from Peoria to the Galena mines crossed the Rock River, boasted a cluster of cabins, as did a few other points along the trail. But much of northern Illinois was trackless prairie, still roamed by Indians. There were no railroads and only a few crude roads. Rivers provided the easiest means of transportation. Truly, New Salem stood on the Illinois frontier.

Always the speculator, Offutt felt that New Salem had potential and decided to open a store when he returned from New Orleans. He was highly impressed with Lincoln's ingenuity in getting the boat over the dam, and hired him on the spot to clerk in the proposed store.

Lincoln returned to New Salem from New Orleans in July of 1831, "a piece of floating driftwood," as he later described himself. He boarded at John Camron's home. While waiting for Offutt, he took on a few odd jobs and piloted a family, bound for Texas, down the Sangamon to Beardstown on a raft. He walked back to New Salem with money in his pocket for the first time in a long while. New Salem held an election on August 1 and Lincoln cast his very first ballot, voting for the Whig Henry Clay for Congress.

When Offutt finally arrived with a stock of goods, he and Lincoln built a cabin to house the store. In September, Abraham Lincoln began a short-lived career as a clerk. His pithy yarns of the Indiana frontier and his steadfast honesty soon made him a popular figure in the village. Once, it is said, he walked six miles to pay back a few cents he had overcharged a woman for dry goods. Another time he walked miles to deliver to a woman four ounces of tea he had under weighed.

Berry-Lincoln General Store, Lincoln's New Salem State Historic Site, Petersburg, IL.

Like most pioneer towns, New Salem's population rose and fell as settlers came, stayed a few months, and moved on. At its peak in 1833, there were perhaps twenty-five families, with a blacksmith, a hatter, a tanner, a cooper, a wheelwright, a tavern, several stores, and a temperance society. There were two doctors, Dr. James Allen, of Vermont, who opened his practice in August 1831, and Dr. Francis Reginer, who arrived from Marrietta, Ohio, in the autumn of 1832. Martin Waddell, the local hatter, went into business that same year. The kettle he used to make felt for his hats can still be seen in the village.

New Salem had no church, but villagers held services in private homes. The village school was a half-mile from town—

taught by Mentor Graham, a self-educated Kentuckian who charged thirty to eighty-five cents per month, depending on the age of the child. Graham's was a "blab" school, where students learned by repeating their lessons aloud, over and over. The school was also used as a church.

Blacksmith, Lincoln's New Salem State Historic Site, Petersburg, IL.

New Salem's homes were not cabins, but fairly substantial and comfortable log houses—by 1830s standards. They had one or two rooms at most; a few had a loft above and all had wooden floors. Home life centered around stone or brick fireplaces, where the cooking was done. Chimneys were built of stone or sticks and logs chinked with mud or plaster. Springfield, with a population of about nine hundred, had a glazier by 1832 and many New Salem homes had glass windows.

Typical of the frontier, New Salem homes became all kitchen at meal time, sitting rooms when neighbors came to call, and parlors on Sunday, when the young men dressed up in their jeans (at the time, any clothes made of heavy, twilled cotton) and the young ladies in their best bow dresses. At night, a house was all bedroom, with both men and women (including visitors and strangers) sleeping on the floor, feet pointed toward the fire.

A woman's life in the frontier villages was not an easy lot and many died at a young age. A foreign traveler described central Illinois as hard country for women and cattle. Families were large and babies came in annual crops. "The fittest survived and the rest the Lord seen fittin' to take away," said one settler.

New Salem's residents were mainly Southerners—from Virginia, Kentucky, Tennessee, and Indiana, with a few Yankees and Easterners thrown in. Some were fairly well educated and had attended Illinois College at Jacksonville, about thirty miles away. Dr. John Allen had a degree from Dartmouth Medical College. Jack Kelso, a "jack of all trades" and homespun philosopher, knew the works of Shakespeare and Burns. James Rutledge, who had a library of twenty-five or thirty volumes, organized a debating society in 1831.

Each family produced most of what it used; nearly all kept a cow. Cash money was scarce and of uncertain value—trade was carried on mainly through long-term credit or barter. Dr. Allen accepted dressed hogs, bacon, and lard in payment of bills.

Lincoln's New Salem State Historic Site, Petersburg, IL.

But if life in New Salem was Spartan, it was not dull. Dances, house-raisings, wolf hunts, militia musters, and camp meetings all became social events. Quilting bees were popular, both men and women taking part (many otherwise rough and tumble pioneer men were quite skilled at quilting). There were horse races, shooting contests, and cock fights. Politics were a preoccupation on the burgeoning frontier. During political campaigns and on the Fourth of July, barbecues were held. Beef and hogs were cooked over a bed of coals prepared days in advance, and then served with turkeys, chickens, pies, and fresh baked bread. Political speeches, games, and contests followed the meal.

New Salem had its rougher element as well, including the Clary's Grove boys, who lived in a crude settlement near the village and hung out at a New Salem store run by Bill Clary. After listening to Denton Offutt brag continually about Lincoln's strength, Jack Armstrong, leader of the gang, challenged him to a wrestling match. Some accounts say Lincoln won, others have the match ending in a draw. Regardless, the event was important to Lincoln's life, for it gave him a reputation for courage and strength and earned him the Clary's Grove boys' respect and support for the rest of his days in New Salem.

By late 1831 Lincoln had become immersed in village life. He joined the debating society and after his first attempt at formal debate, the society's president remarked, ". . . there was more than wit and fun in Abe's head." With Mentor Graham's help, Lincoln began to study grammar and mathematics. The association with more highly educated people expanded his horizons.

The year 1832 brought events important both to the village and to Abraham Lincoln's future. From the very beginning, New Salem's settlers had hoped the town's Sangamon River location would make it a major port. In March of 1832, the Talisman, a small, light draft steamer, made it up the river as far as Portland Landing, several miles above New Salem. But then, as now, the Sangamon's levels fluctuated widely. As the river dropped, Rowan Herndon, who was an experienced boatman, was hired to pilot the Talisman back to the safety of the Illinois River. He hired Lincoln as his assistant—the job paid forty dollars—and they maneuvered the vessel back to Beardstown only with great difficulty. New Salem's port city dreams held on as long as the village existed, but the reality died aborning in 1832.

That same month Lincoln, who had decided years earlier in Indiana that he wanted to make a living with his mind and not his muscles, announced his candidacy for the Illinois legislature.

He ran as a Whig candidate—his political idol was the Kentuckian Henry Clay—and he was a strong believer in internal improvements and firmly against the practice of loaning money at exorbitant rates of interest. He concluded a political handbill he had written with the words: "I am young and unknown to many of you. I was born and have ever remained in the most humble walks of life. I have no wealthy or powerful relations or friends to recommend me. My case is thrown exclusively on the independent voters of the county; and, if elected, they will have conferred a favor upon me, for which I shall be unremitting in my labors to compensate. But if the good people in their wisdom shall see fit to keep me in the background, I have been too familiar with disappointments to be very much chagrined . . ." Shortly after the announcement, Offutt's store failed and Lincoln was without work.

In April, a wave of fear and excitement swept New Salem as the Sauk leader Black Hawk crossed the Mississippi from Iowa and returned to his former tribal village near present-day Rock Island. With him was a party of twelve hundred Sauk and Fox Indians who came ostensibly to plant corn, but there were nearly five hundred warriors in the group, mounted and well armed. Governor John Reynolds issued an urgent call for volunteers for the state militia. Political considerations aside, Lincoln borrowed a horse and joined up.

The rag-tag New Salem contingent assembled at Richland Creek, nine miles southwest of the village, then marched to Beardstown where the company was sworn into state service and the Clary's Grove boys elected Lincoln company captain. Years later Lincoln wrote that he was "surprised" at the election and had "not since had any success in life which gave him so much satisfaction." At Beardstown, Lincoln's company became part of a mounted brigade, then moved to the mouth of the Rock River to be sworn into Federal service.

Enlistments in the military were short, thirty days or less, and Lincoln reenlisted three times, serving in the Black Hawk War for a total of fifty-one days without seeing action. But following the Battle of Stillman's Run, at present-day Stillman Valley, Illinois, he helped bury several of General Isaiah Stillman's men just killed in a sharp skirmish. For a long time after he remembered how "the red light of the morning sun was streaming upon them as they lay heads toward us on the ground." During the four-month war that claimed some two hundred soldiers and settlers, and more than a thousand Indians, Lincoln served with many men whose paths he would cross in later life—General Zachary Taylor, who became the nation's twelfth president; Lieutenant Robert Anderson, who had the misfortune to be in command of Fort Sumter when the Civil War broke out; Lieutenant Jefferson Davis, later President of the Confederacy; Lieutenant Albert Sidney Johnson, who became one of the Confederacy's finest generals; and others who were later governors, senators, and statesmen.

Lincoln mustered out of service at Whitewater, Wisconsin, (then Michigan Territory) on July 10, three weeks before the war ended. His horse had been stolen the day before, and he walked most of the way home to New Salem. For his service, Lincoln received $125 and a land grant in Iowa Territory in present-day Tama and Crawford Counties.

He arrived in New Salem in late July, just two weeks before the election, and campaigned vigorously, introducing himself to farmers and often lending a hand with the field work. But Lincoln lost the election, finishing eighth in a field of thirteen candidates campaigning for four legislative seats. It was the only time the people rejected his bid for office. Despite the loss, the political fires that simmered within him had been fanned to a bright flame.

During his six years in New Salem, Lincoln eked out his living in many ways, not all of them successful. Following the failure of Offutt's store, he entered into an ill-destined partnership in a store with William Berry that put him deeply in debt for many years. From 1833 until 1836, Lincoln was New Salem's postmaster, a job that paid about fifty dollars a year and provided free mailing privileges. He avidly read every newspaper that came through the office and often kept the mail in his hat. On occasion, he simply left the post office unlocked and patrons picked up their own mail. At various times Lincoln split rails, helped at the mill, worked as a farmhand, and served as the local agent for the *Sangamo Journal*, a newspaper published in Springfield. He clerked at New Salem's elections, earning two dollars and fifty cents for carrying the tally sheets the twenty miles to Springfield.

Lincoln secured an appointment as deputy county surveyor in

the fall of 1833 and learned how to survey by reading books. He marked out farm boundaries, surveyed roads (some still in use), and plotted several towns, including New Boston, Petersburg, Bath, Albany, and Huron. Huron and Albany were towns in name only; the others are still in existence. (The present Albany, Illinois, in Whiteside County, is not the Albany that Lincoln surveyed.)

Lincoln owned no home in New Salem, but boarded with various families in the village or at the Rutledge Tavern. It was there he met Ann Rutledge, and his relationship with her has become part of the Lincoln legend. The daughter of town founder and innkeeper James Rutledge, Ann was born in Kentucky in 1813. Described as pretty and slight, with blue eyes and auburn hair, she was engaged to John McNamar when Lincoln met her. The Rutledges moved to a farm at Sand Ridge, seven miles north of New Salem, in 1833, and Lincoln was a frequent visitor as he traveled the county as a surveyor. In the summer of 1835, Ann contracted a fever and died at age twenty-two. The normally melancholy Lincoln took her death unusually hard. That much is known fact.

By the time Lincoln became President, his relationship with Ann Rutledge, whatever it may have been, was largely forgotten. But in 1862, accounts published in Petersburg had Lincoln courting the fair Ann in earnest, proposing and finally winning her heart and hand. According to Lincoln's third law partner and biographer, William Herndon, Lincoln had a final, poignant hour with Ann as she lay on her death bed, and was grief stricken when she died. It is said that he talked wildly and incoherently, claiming his heart was buried with Ann, and telling one friend the thought "that the snows and rains fell upon her grave filled him with indescribable grief." He lived in seclusion with the Bowling Green family for a time and Ann's memory is supposed to have influenced the rest of Lincoln's life. Although he later married, myth claims the beautiful Ann was Lincoln's one and only love.

"Where there's smoke, there's fire," as they say on the prairie, but many historians now that think Herndon blew the relationship out of proportion, perhaps stressing the romance in his biography of Lincoln to strike out at Lincoln's wife, for whom he had a strong dislike. The feelings were mutual on her part. Quite likely the Lincoln-Rutledge relationship fell somewhere between a proposal of marriage and a casual friendship. Regardless, the tale has been embellished over the years and is enshrined in Lincoln folklore. Ann Rutledge is buried near New Salem (see Petersburg, Illinois).

Lincoln's prospects soared in 1834 when he again ran as a Whig candidate and was elected to the state legislature. He borrowed two hundred dollars from Coleman Smoot, a well-to-do farmer, spent sixty dollars on a new suit, paid a debt or two, and took a stage to his first legislative session in the then state capital of Vandalia.

In Vandalia, John T. Stuart, a Springfield attorney and fellow Sangamon County legislator who had served with Lincoln in the Black Hawk War, urged him to study law. His interest in law from the Indiana days revived, Lincoln rode, or sometimes walked, to Springfield to borrow books from Stuart. Between legislative sessions he studied constantly and was often seen often lying on his back in the shade of a tree, his long legs propped against the trunk, his face buried in a law book. At times he studied in Henry Onstot's cooper shop, feeding the fire with wood shavings as he read late into the night.

There were no state bar exams and only one law school west of the Appalachians, but Lincoln learned enough to be licensed to practice on September 9, 1836, after the Sangamon Circuit Court gave him a certificate of good character. Exams, if any, were informal and given by practicing attorneys, an occasion usually followed by the candidate taking his examiners to dinner. Lincoln argued his first case in Springfield a short time later, substituting for his mentor, John Stuart. In three related cases that were settled out of court, Lincoln lost on one count and got settlements on two.

Lincoln returned to New Salem following the 1836-37 legislative session, but he saw no future here. Springfield was now the new state capital—Lincoln had helped legislate the move in the legislative session just ended—and he stayed in New Salem only long enough to pack his bags and say his farewells. On April 15 he moved to Springfield to become John Stuart's law partner. The New Salem days were over. Lincoln first came to the frontier village a gawky, rough, uneducated twenty-one-year-old. He left as a qualified lawyer and a growing power in state politics.

Like many pioneer villages, New Salem's life span was short.

Nearby Petersburg, founded in 1832, began to usurp New Salem's role as a trade center by the mid 1830s. New Salem lost its post office to Petersburg in 1836. When the now thriving Petersburg became the seat of newly-established Menard County in 1839, New Salem's few remaining residents moved on. By late 1840, New Salem had ceased to exist. At the time of Lincoln's death, in 1865, only one lonely log cabin remained here. A few years later even that was gone.

But as the Lincoln legend grew, New Salem was never quite forgotten. Newspaper publisher William Randolph Hearst purchased the land where the village once stood and in 1906 presented it to the Old Salem Chautauqua Association. In 1917, the people of Petersburg organized the Old Salem League and, with the help of pioneer settlers, located several home sites and roads. The site was presented to the State of Illinois to develop as a state park in 1919.

After years of extensive research and archaeological investigation, the recreation of New Salem began in 1932. The initial construction ran into the 1940s and research, with occasional additions to the village, continues to this day.

To gain insights into New Salem, stop first at the Visitor Center, which houses an auditorium, a museum, original Lincoln items, items used in New Salem during Lincoln's time there, and a fascinating "time walk" that takes you through village history, from founding to reconstruction. A short film, "Turning Point, Lincoln's New Salem," is offered, along with various workshops and a lecture series.

Prominently displayed in the museum is the surveyor's compass and chain with which Lincoln plotted towns, farms, and roads while he was the deputy surveyor of Sangamon County. There's also a ladderback chair he is said to have repaired, and a doll he brought from Beardstown to a friend's daughter.

Near the Visitor Center is the Lincoln League Concession Stand, offering gifts, souvenirs, a good selection of Lincoln Books, and a McDonald's Express fast food restaurant; closed November through March, tel. 217-632-2277.

In the village you'll find twelve log houses, the Rutledge Tavern, ten workshops, stores, mills, and a school where church services were held. Only one—the restored Henry Onstot Cooper

Shop, discovered in Petersburg in 1922 and moved back to its original site—stood here in Lincoln's time. The others have been meticulously reproduced as they were in the 1830s. Most stand on their original sites. The furnishings are authentic. More than nine hundred artifacts in the buildings include wheat cradles, candle molds, cord beds, flax shuttles, wool cards, dough and cornmeal chests, and early American pewter. Many items were actually used by New Salem people in the 1830s.

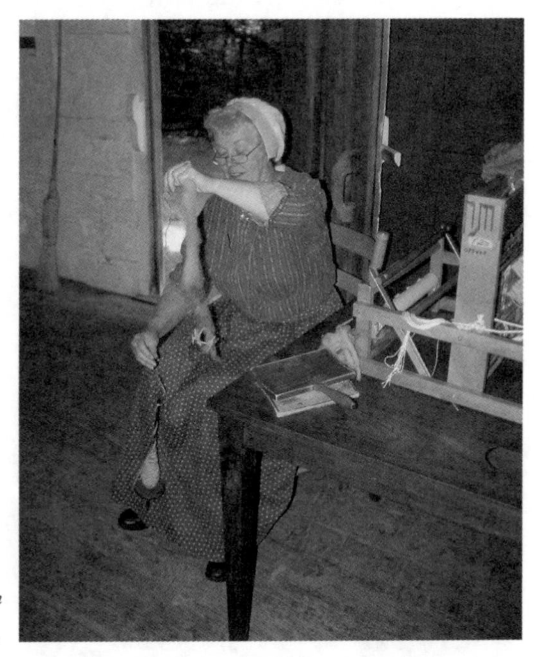

Spinning yarn, Lincoln's New Salem State Historic Site, Petersburg, IL.

Interpreters in period dress demonstrate 1830s chores and home life at several village homes and businesses—dipping candles, cooking, blacksmithing, making lye soap, weaving rugs and cloth.

An archaeology walk located behind the second Lincoln-Berry store features the remains of two previously unknown home sites discovered in 1995, along with a road that crossed the hilltop. On site displays describe the remains found here. A remnant of the old road can also be seen.

The Lincoln League Museum Store, located near the Rutledge Tavern in a stone building not part of the original village, offers nineteenth-century craft reproductions by Illinois artisans; closed November through March, tel. 217-632-3443.

Special events held at New Salem during the year include story telling, traditional music festivals, candlelight tours, and a harvest feast. Events and dates vary.

Tours of New Salem are self-guided—a brochure with a map and profiles of the buildings and the people who lived here is available free at the Visitor Center.

You can cover New Salem's highlights in a hurried hour, but you would cheat yourself by doing so. Take time to watch the demonstrations and talk to the interpreters; they can add much to your visit.

New Salem State Park: The park has picnic areas with water, tables, fireplaces, and a small shelter adjacent to the historic village. Admission is free. A park campground has sites for both tents and recreational vehicles, electrical hookups, a sanitary station, and modern restrooms with showers. A fee is charged for camping. The modern restrooms and showers are closed November 15 to April 1.

Above: "Lincoln, Book, and Ax," by Arvaard Fairbanks, New Salem State Park.

Left: "Lincoln on the Prairie," by Anna Hyatt Huntington, New Salem State Park.

There are two Lincoln statues in the park. "Lincoln on the Prairie," by Anna Hyatt Huntington, depicts Lincoln reading a book while astride a grazing horse. The statue, at the park entrance on Route 97, was exhibited at the New York World's Fair of 1939. "Lincoln, Book, and Ax," by Arvaard Fairbanks, portrays a resolute young Lincoln, book in one hand, ax in the other. Donated to New Salem by the descendants of the Mormon Pioneers of Utah, the statue stands next to the New Salem Visitor Center.

THEATER IN THE PARK: A variety of live productions are offered from mid-June through late August in the outdoor Kelso Hollow Amphitheater, located behind the Visitors Center; tel. 217/632-4000.

Mentor Graham grave site, Petersburg, IL.

Nearby Related Sites:

MENTOR GRAHAM GRAVESITE: "I think I may say that he was my scholar and I was his teacher," said the New Salem schoolteacher of the man he helped with his studies of grammar and mathematics. In a letter to William Herndon in 1865, Graham said that Lincoln lived with him for about six months in 1833. Ann Rutledge was also his pupil. Graham taught in various rural Illinois schools until he was seventy-nine and died in South Dakota in 1886, at the age of eighty-six. His remains were returned to Illinois in 1933 and interred in the Farmer's Point Cemetery, two miles south of New Salem on Route 97.

WILLIAM BERRY GRAVESITE: William Berry was a corporal in Captain Abraham Lincoln's company in the Black Hawk War and was Lincoln's partner in a store at New Salem in 1832 and 1833. When Berry died, in 1835 at age twenty-four, Lincoln assumed the debts of the business, which took him years to pay off. Berry is buried in the cemetery of Rock Creek Cumberland Presbyterian Church which his father founded in 1822. A marker on Route 97, five miles south of New Salem, commemorates the spot.

Petersburg, Illinois (pop. 2,200) Menard County

Two miles below New Salem on the Sangamon River, Petersburg was founded in 1832 by Peter Lukins and George Warbuton, both of whom had been New Salem residents. Tradition says that Warbuton and Lukins, each wanting the town named after himself, played a game of cards for the honor of selecting the name. Lukins won, so the village was named Petersburg, instead of Georgetown for George Warbuton. But Petersburg failed and the owners sold out to John Taylor, of Springfield, who hired Lincoln to re-survey the village on February 17, 1836. It is said that Lincoln ran one street crooked in order to preserve the home of a widow whose husband he had served with in the Black Hawk War.

Lincoln maintained strong ties with Petersburg for many years. From 1839 to 1847, Menard County was part of the Eighth Judicial Circuit, and Lincoln returned to Petersburg each spring and fall when court was in session. He spoke in the village during various political campaigns. The convention which nominated Lincoln as a candidate for Congress met in Petersburg on May 1, 1846. In the 1850s, his strong anti-slavery speeches drew boos here.

Lincoln survey marker, Petersburg, IL.

LINCOLN SURVEY POINT: The spot where Lincoln began his 1836 survey of the village is marked by a plaque set in the pavement at the corner of 7th and Jackson Streets on the village square.

MENARD COUNTY COURTHOUSE: Many documents related to Lincoln's law practice are displayed on the second floor of the courthouse. These include a short will Lincoln wrote for a friend before he was admitted to the bar, and forty-seven other legal papers written by him, including a writ of execution, subpoenas, a bill of complaint, and other documents. The courthouse is located on the village square and is open Monday-Friday 8:30-4:30; closed Saturday-Sunday and holidays. Admission: Free. Additional information: Tel. 217-632-7363.

ROSE HILL CEMETERY: The cemetery, one mile east of Petersburg on Route 123, contains the graves of Major B. F. Stevenson, founder of the Grand Army of the Republic; Peter Lukins, for whom Petersburg was named; and Dr. John Allen and Samuel Hill of New Salem fame.

OAKLAND CEMETERY: Ann Rutledge was originally buried in Concord Cemetery, but in 1890 her body, or remains that passed for it, was reinterred in Oakland Cemetery, on the southwest edge of Petersburg. The stone marking her grave bears an inscription by Illinois poet Edgar Lee Masters, who is buried nearby. Here too are the graves of "Mitch" Miller, Hannah Armstrong, and Bowling and Nancy Green, all of whom Lincoln knew in New Salem. Upon entering the cemetery, turn right at the second lane to reach the Rutledge grave.

Ann Rutledge grave, Petersburg, IL.

Other Petersburg Attractions:

Edgar Lee Masters Home: The famed Illinois poet, best known for his Spoon River Anthology, spent much of his boyhood in Petersburg. His restored boyhood home features memorabilia of his life, some original furnishings, and copies of his more than fifty works. Located at the corner of 8th and Jackson Streets, the home is open 10-12 and 1-3, Tuesday and Thursday-Saturday, Memorial Day through Labor Day; closed the rest of the year. Admission: Free. Additional information: tel. 217-632-7363.

Menard County Historical Museum: The museum displays changing architectural, archaeological, and historical exhibits of coal mining tools, military clothing and equipment, photos, and documents. Genealogical and historical records are open to researchers. Located on the village square, the museum is open 8:30-1:30, Monday, Wednesday, and Friday. Admission: Free. Additional information: Menard County Historical Museum, 125 S. 7th Street, Petersburg, IL 62675; tel. 217-632-7363.

Nearby Accommodations:

The Oaks, 510 W. Sheridan, Petersburg, IL 62675, offers bed and breakfast accommodations in a restored 1875 Italianate mansion; tel. 217-632-5444 or 1-888-724-6257. www.petersburgil.com/accommodations/the_oaks.html

Gilmores Café, 501 S. Sixth, tel. 217-632-3816.

Stonebake, 221 E. Douglas, tel. 217-632-2461.

Additional Information:
Petersburg Chamber of Commerce, 125 S. 7th Street,
Petersburg, IL 62675; tel. 217-632-7363.
www.petersburgil.com/

VANDALIA STATEHOUSE STATE HISTORIC SITE
Vandalia, Illinois

Vandalia Statehouse State Historic Site, Vandalia, IL.

LOCATION: Fourth and Gallatin Streets on Route 140; Fayette County.

HOURS: Open daily 8:30-5, March-October, 8-4, November-February; closed New Year's Day, Martin Luther King, Jr. Birthday, Veterans Day, General Election Day, Thanksgiving, and Christmas.

ADMISSION: Suggested donation.

ACCESSIBILITY: Three steps into building; lower level wheelchair accessible with assistance.

Information: Vandalia Statehouse State Historic Site, 315 W. Gallatin, Vandalia, IL 62471; tel. 618-283-1161. www.state.il.us/hpa/

Getting There: Vandalia is 70 miles northeast of St. Louis, 35 miles southwest of Effingham via I-70.

Set on the banks of the Kaskaskia River, Vandalia was the second capital of Illinois, holding that honor from 1820 to 1839. (The first Illinois capital, 1818 to 1820, was the village of Kaskaskia, on the banks of the Mississippi eighty-five miles below St. Louis.) Vandalia stands at the western terminus of the uncompleted National Road, and was carved out of the wilderness in 1819 as the northerly shift of Illinois' increasing population necessitated moving the capital.

The present vernacular Federal-style statehouse is the third capitol built at Vandalia. The first, a two-story frame building erected in 1820, was destroyed by fire in 1823. The remodeled Old State Bank replaced it in 1824, but by the time Lincoln was elected to the legislature, the two-story brick building was in an advanced state of deterioration. By 1836 there were fears it would actually collapse. It was razed and the present statehouse was constructed in less than four months time.

What Happened Here

Abraham Lincoln first saw Vandalia from the seat of a rumbling stagecoach whose driver dramatically blew a horn to signal the end of the seventy-five-mile, thirty-six-hour journey from New Salem. Normally quiet, the backwater of some nine hundred people sprang to life when the legislature convened. Legislators, jurists, and lobbyists crowded the plank sidewalks, carriages and coaches rumbled through the rutted, muddy streets, and the taverns and inns hummed with conversation and the clink of glasses.

Lincoln took it all in as he shared a room with John T. Stuart, of Springfield, the Whig floorleader. Through Stuart, Lincoln met the legislators, lawyers, and favor-seekers who controlled Illinois politics. One such was Stephen A. Douglas, of Jacksonville, in Morgan County. A Democrat who had come to the state capital promoting his candidacy for state's attorney of the First

Judicial District, Douglas stood only five feet four inches tall, had massive shoulders, a barrel chest, heavy brows set above piercing eyes, and a general air of belligerence. Originally from Vermont, he had lived in Illinois less than two years, but was already such a force in state politics that he was known as the "Little Giant." It is said that after meeting Douglas, the six foot, four inch Lincoln described him as "the least man he had ever seen." The two were to be fierce political adversaries for decades. Their famous debates, held twenty-four years later, thrust Lincoln into the national political spotlight (see Lincoln-Douglas debates).

When the 1834 legislative session opened, Lincoln took his place in the House of Representative chambers on the first floor of the old bank building. Members sat at long tables, three to a table. A fireplace and stove provided warmth. Candles in tall holders provided dim light for evening sessions. There was a common water pail with tin dippers; boxes of sand served as cuspidors. The crash of falling plaster occasionally interrupted the proceedings.

Internal improvements—the development of roads, ferries, bridges, and railroads—were important issues in the Ninth General Assembly. Lincoln introduced bills to authorize a toll bridge over Salt Creek near New Salem, and to locate a road from Springfield to Miller's Ferry on the Sangamon River, twelve miles northwest of New Salem. But for the most part, he watched and listened and learned.

When the session ended, in February 1835, Lincoln was paid $258 for his services and traveling expenses. He returned to New Salem in sub-zero temperatures and, encouraged by Stuart, took up his study of the law in earnest.

Lincoln was reelected in 1836 and 1838 and served in the legislature at a time when some of the most important measures in the state's history were discussed and debated in Vandalia. Slavery was one vital issue and much was accomplished in Vandalia that resulted in Illinois becoming a free state. The first Illinois school laws were enacted in Vandalia, the highly controversial State Bank was debated here, as was the $10 million internal improvements acts for railroads and transportation systems.

During a special legislative session that ran from December 1835 to February 1836, the Democrats held the first political convention in Illinois. Spearheaded by Douglas, the party chose a uniform slate of candidates and drafted a platform that all Democrats were pledged to support or be expelled from the party. The Whigs emphatically opposed the convention system, calling it a menace to liberty and republican government. Lincoln was instrumental in the anti-convention fight as the Whigs swore to retain the system where anyone could run for office by simply announcing his candidacy.

When the Tenth General Assembly convened in Vandalia on December 5, 1836, the legislature met in the new statehouse, although it was far from completed and the plaster was still wet. Douglas was now a member of the legislature and Lincoln had become the acknowledged floorleader of the Whigs. The city of Chicago was incorporated during this session. Lincoln voted against a series of resolutions declaring that the Constitution sanctified the right of property in slaves, that slavery was wholly within the jurisdiction of the states, and that the Federal government had no right to abolish it in the District of Columbia, but the resolutions passed, seventy-seven to six. In January 1837, Lincoln made his first published speech in opposition to an attack on the State Bank of Illinois.

Following an 1835 census, the legislature was reapportioned. Sangamon County now had nine representatives—seven in the house and two in the state senate. All were Whigs, and all stood six feet or taller. Collectively, they were known as the "Long Nine."

With the Illinois population continuing to shift northward, there were increasing calls to move the seat of government. Springfield had long hoped to be the site of the capital, but southern Illinois legislators strongly opposed relocation. However, reapportionment had shifted the balance of power and, with the Long Nine leading the way, a rough and tumble battle to relocate the capital ensued. When the dust settled, Springfield had won. It became the new state capital on July 4, 1839.

The Eleventh General Assembly, which convened in December 1838, was the last held in Vandalia.

In all, Lincoln spent some forty-four weeks as a temporary resident of Vandalia. Here he learned the inner workings of government, began his study of law, and was admitted to the bar. In barely five years, he grew from backwoods politician to respected political leader, and had become one of the movers and shakers in the Whig party. He had come a long way from stump speeches in New Salem.

The last legislative session in Vandalia conveyed the statehouse to Fayette County and the town of Vandalia, to be used jointly as a school and courthouse. The county took over the building in 1856 and the old statehouse served as the Fayette County Courthouse until 1933. Restoration of the building began at that time.

Representative's Room (1836), Vandalia Statehouse State Historic Site, Vandalia, IL.

The white-painted brick statehouse stands on a pleasant square in the center of Vandalia. In the lower level are the Supreme Court Chambers and the offices of Secretary of State, State Auditor, Public Accounts, and State Treasurer, all furnished with period pieces. The Supreme Court Chambers hold a judge's bench and four seats, with attorneys' and clerks' tables clustered before the bench, and pew-like benches for spectators.

Legislators' desks in the upper level of the House of Representatives each seat three, just as in Lincoln's day, while the Senate chamber is furnished with individual desks. Each has inkwells, quill pens, and pewter candleholders. There are large candelabras in each chamber, and sand-filled wooden cuspidors.

Tours of the Vandalia Statehouse are self-guided. Special events include The Grand Levee (second weekend in June), with demonstrations of period arts and crafts and candlelight tours of the old capitol. Christmas candlelight tours are given on the second Sunday in December, when the historic building is decorated for the season.

Vandalia, Illinois (pop. 6,200)

While many of the buildings that surrounded the Statehouse Square in Lincoln's time are gone, historical markers indicate the locations of several, including the first and second capitols, the office of the Public Printer, and the home of Governor L. D. Ewing. A brochure and map showing important historical sites is available from the Chamber of Commerce. A Lincoln Trail Marker in Rogier Park, west on Fillmore Street, marks the site of the route Lincoln took on his trips between Vandalia and Springfield.

Madonna of the Trail: One of twelve statues erected by the National Society of the Daughters of the of the American Revolution to mark the route of the Old National Road (Cumberland Trail), the monument depicts a pioneer mother with a child clinking to her skirt and another cradled in her arms. It stands at the corner of Fourth and Gallatin Streets, near the statehouse grounds, marking the western terminus of the National Road. The eighty-foot-wide road ran for 591 miles from Cumberland, Maryland to Vandalia. It was never completed.

Fayette County Museum: Housed in the century-old former First Presbyterian Church, the museum has exhibits and artifacts dating back to Vandalia's days as the state capital. Located at Main and Kennedy Streets, the museum is open Monday-Saturday 9-4:30, Sunday 1-4, June through August, with limited hours the rest of the year. Admission: Free.

Nearby Accommodations:

Days Inn of Vandalia (93 rooms), 1920 Kennedy Blvd. US 51 N./I-70 Exit 63, Vandalia, IL 62471, tel. 618-283-4400.

Ramada Limited (60 rooms) 2727 Van Tran Avenue I-70 Exit 61, Vandalia, IL 62471, tel. 618-283-1000.

The Depot, 107 S. Sixth Street, tel. 618-283-1918.

Ponderosa, I-70 Exit 61, tel. 618-283-4559.

Additional Information:
Vandalia Chamber of Commerce, 1408 N. Fifth Street, P.O. Box 238, Vandalia, IL 62471; tel. 618-283-2728. www.vandalia.net/

A tourist information center is located at the junction of I-70 and U.S. 51.

THE ABRAHAM LINCOLN LONG NINE MUSEUM

Athens, Illinois

LOCATION: 200 S. Main, Athens; Menard County.

HOURS: Open Tuesday-Saturday 1-5, June 1-September, closed Sunday, Monday, and July 4.

ADMISSION: Adults $2; ages 6-12 $1; ages 5 and under free.

ACCESSIBILITY: Ground floor, with assistance.

INFORMATION: Long Nine Museum, P.O. Box 362, Athens, IL 62613, tel. 217-636-8755. www.abelincoln.com/long9/

GETTING THERE: Athens is located seven miles east of Lincoln's New Salem on the old Post Road and twelve miles north of Springfield on Highway 29.

Athens (pronounced A-thens) dates from 1831, when Matthew Rogers, an early settler, built a two-story frame building to house a general store and post office; the upper level was used as a meeting room.

In November, 1834, Lincoln relocated a portion of the road between Sangamontown and Athens, receiving $3.00 for one day's surveying labor and fifty cents for a map. The survey marker Lincoln placed in the road at Athens can still be seen in the intersection next to the museum. In 1836, Lincoln opened a series of ten speaking engagements in Athens in his campaign for reelection to the Illinois legislature and, several years later, represented Matthew Rogers in litigation to reprocess the general store building when the second owner defaulted on his payments.

Lincoln survey marker, Athens, IL.

What Happened Here

On August 3, 1837, the citizens of Athens (then located in Sangamon County) gave a public dinner on the second floor of Rogers' general store in appreciation to the Sangamon County "Long Nine"—the legislators who spearheaded the move of the Illinois capital to Springfield. Seven of the nine attended, including Lincoln, who was toasted as "One of nature's nobility." Lincoln responded, saying, "Sangamon County will ever be true to her best interest and never so than in reciprocating the good feeling of the citizens of Athens and neighborhood."

Two years later, the Sangamon County boundaries were redrawn and Athens became part of the new Menard County.

The wood-frame building Colonel Matthew Rogers built in 1832 still stands, saved from destruction in the 1970s by a group of concerned citizens. The restored building is now a museum with a replica of Rogers' general store and post office (where some of the original flooring can be seen), and documentation of the historic building's background. The second floor contains dioramas that tell the story of Abraham Lincoln in Athens and recreates the banquet scene, using antiques and period reproductions. The exhibit highlight is a large oil painting of the banquet room by the late Lloyd Ostendorf, showing Lincoln in formal dress toasting his colleagues.

Top Right: Abraham Lincoln, in the personage of re-enactor Charlie Ott, Athens, IL, on the 160th anniversary of the "Long Nine."

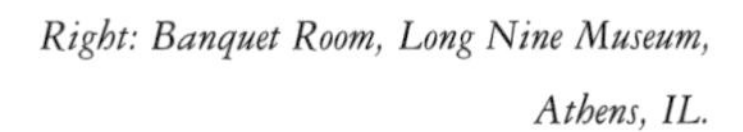

Top Left: Colonel William Rogers Building (1831-32), Athens, IL, home of the Long Nine Museum.

Right: Banquet Room, Long Nine Museum, Athens, IL.

Nearby Accommodations:
See Petersburg or Springfield, Illinois.

"Well, Speed, I'm moved."

A. Lincoln 1837

Springfield, Illinois

Old State Capitol State Historic Site, Springfield, IL.

Location: Central Illinois; Sangamon County.

Admission: All Springfield Lincoln sites are free.

Accessibility: Varies; the Convention and Visitors Bureau offers a brochure detailing wheelchair accessibility at all sites, including many hotels and motels.

Information: Springfield Convention & Visitors Bureau, 109 N. 7th Street, Springfield, IL 62701; tel. 800-545-7300 or 217-789-2360. www.visit-springfieldillinois.com/

Getting There: Springfield is 95 miles northeast of St. Louis, 200 miles southwest of Chicago via I-55.

The business of government is the business of this prairie capital of 112,000 and, as in Lincoln's day, Springfield comes to life when the Illinois legislature is in session. Lawyers, lobbyists, and favor-seekers flock to the capital, the sidewalks bustle with state workers hurrying to and fro, restaurants and watering holes hum with political conversation and the clink of glasses—that part of the scenario has changed little since 1839.

Most of the Lincoln sites are clustered in the center of Springfield, within easy walking distance of each other. The city's one-way street system is easy to navigate and routes to historic sites are well-marked. Springfield draws more than a million visitors each year, most to take in the Lincoln sites, so you can anticipate lots of company from late spring through fall. Dining and lodging accommodations are good, and plentiful, although if your visit coincides with the Illinois State Fair, held the second week of August, advance lodging reservations are recommended. The city offers many attractions beyond its Lincoln sites, with special events held throughout the year.

What Happened Here

Springfield in 1837 had changed from the raw town Abraham Lincoln first saw in the spring of 1831. Boasting a population of two thousand and a smattering of new brick buildings, it had more than two dozen stores, six churches, eleven lawyers, and eighteen doctors. The town was on the move—its selection as state capital had assured its future—but traces of its frontier beginnings remained. A public whipping post stood on the east side of the public square and hogs and cows ran loose through the rough, muddy streets.

Lincoln's first stop in Springfield was at Joshua Speed's general store where he sought lodging. When Speed offered to share his own room above the store, Lincoln took his saddlebags upstairs, came down, and said, "Well, Speed, I'm moved." That same day the *Sangamo Journal*, Springfield's Whig newspaper, carried the following notice: "J. T. Stuart and A. Lincoln, Attorneys and Counsellors at Law, will practice conjointly in the courts of this Judicial Circuit. Office No. 4 Hoffman's Row upstairs. Springfield, April 12, 1837."

Lincoln ran the firm alone for much of the time while Stuart served a term in the U.S. Congress. On the day Stuart left for Washington, Lincoln began a fresh page in the firm's account book headed: "Commencement of Lincoln's administration, 1839. Nov. 2." And each time Stuart returned to Springfield, Lincoln handed him envelopes containing one-half of the proceeds from various cases he'd handled.

During his three years with Stuart, Lincoln divided his time between the law and the legislature. He began riding the Eighth Judicial Circuit in 1839, going on the road each spring and autumn to try cases throughout the central and eastern parts of the state (see Eighth Judicial Circuit). He was admitted into practice before the U.S. Circuit and District Courts when those offices were moved from Vandalia to Springfield in 1839, and within two years had tried seven cases before the Illinois Supreme Court. Pursuing his political career, Lincoln ran for, and was reelected to, the state legislature in 1838 and 1840, serving in the last legislative session held in Vandalia and the first held in Springfield.

When the Stuart-Lincoln partnership ended amicably in 1841, Lincoln joined the firm of Stephen T. Logan. After three years, he left Logan and took William H. Herndon as a partner.

The Lincoln-Herndon partnership was a strange alliance. They had met in New Salem in 1832 and roomed together at Speed's store when Herndon was a clerk there. As different as day and night, they apparently got along well. Both were Whigs—Lincoln was a conservative and a teetotaler, Herndon a radical and heavy drinker. Lincoln, ten years older, called Herndon "Billy," but Herndon always addressed his partner as "Mr. Lincoln."

Why Lincoln chose him remains a mystery. "I confess I was surprised when he invited me to become his partner," Herndon later wrote. As to why, Herndon said, "I don't know and no one else does." Herndon managed the office and did much of the legal research, while Lincoln traveled the Eighth Judicial Circuit. Both argued cases in court and split their fees equally. The partnership lasted for twenty-one years, until the day John Wilkes Booth fired the shot that took Lincoln's life, although Herndon saw Lincoln only once after he became President.

Lincoln was romantically involved with three women in his lifetime—Ann Rutledge, whom he knew in New Salem (see

New Salem, Illinois), Mary Owens, and Mary Todd, the woman he married.

Lincoln met Mary Owens in New Salem in 1833, when she came from Kentucky to visit her sister, Mrs. Bennett Abell. She stayed only a month, but apparently impressed Lincoln. In 1836, a year after Ann Rutledge's death, Mrs. Abell went to Kentucky to return the visit and told Lincoln, in an apparent lighted-hearted vein, that she would bring Mary back if he would marry her. Lincoln agreed—it is assumed his tone was equally lighthearted—and when Mrs. Abell returned to New Salem in November 1836, Mary Owens came with her. Was Lincoln pleasantly surprised? His reaction is not known, but letters he wrote suggest a romantic involvement. Still, while Mary Owens remained in New Salem until the spring of 1838, Lincoln spent the four months from December 1836 to March 1837 at the legislative session in Vandalia, and moved from New Salem to Springfield in April 1837. They were seldom seen together.

Letters Lincoln wrote Mary also indicate a confused and unhappy relationship. On December 13, 1836, he wrote from Vandalia, saying he had "not been pleased since I left you." Writing from Springfield on May 7, 1837, Lincoln said that he had torn up two letters he'd started and that "I am often thinking about what we said about your coming to live at Springfield. There is a great deal of flourishing about in carriages here, which it would be your doom to see without sharing in it. You would have to be poor, without the means of hiding your poverty." Then, on August 16, the same day he parted from her, Lincoln wrote "If you feel yourself in any degree bound to me, I am now willing to release you, provided you wish it; while on the other hand, I am willing and even anxious to bind you faster, if I can be convinced that it will, in any considerable degree, add to your happiness . . . If it suits you best not to answer this—farewell—a long life and a merry one attend you. But if you conclude to write back, speak plainly as I do . . ." The letter was signed, "Your friend, Lincoln."

Whether or not it was intended as a "Dear Mary" letter, it served that purpose. Mary Owens did not answer; Lincoln never saw her again. When William Herndon, preparing his biography of Lincoln, contacted her about the affair in 1866, Mary, then married and the mother of several children, replied, "I thought

Mr. Lincoln was deficient in those little links which make up the chain of woman's happiness—at least it was so in my case."

Lincoln met Mary Todd in Springfield during a party at the home of her sister and brother-in-law, Elizabeth and Ninian Edwards, in December 1839. A Kentuckian from a prominent Lexington family, Mary Todd was twenty-one years old, well educated, and moved easily in the city's highest social circles. She was five feet two, plump in the fashion of the day, and had a turned up nose that Lincoln liked.

Lincoln became a regular caller at the Edward's and he and Mary Todd began courting. By the end of 1840, they were engaged to be married. But Ninian and Elizabeth Edwards stepped in and tried to break up the romance. Social distinctions were important to them. Mary Todd came from a proud and educated family, and Ninian Edwards, who had been a member of the Long Nine with Lincoln in the Illinois legislature, considered him a "rough" man whose background and social position were inferior. They announced that Lincoln was no longer welcome at their home.

On what Lincoln called the "fatal first of Jany. '41," the engagement was broken. Devastated, Lincoln sank into a deep depression. He struggled through the legislative session, which adjourned in March, and avoided contact with Mary, although letters he wrote to friends indicate he thought about her constantly.

In the summer of 1842, Mrs. Simeon Francis, wife of the editor of the *Sangamo Journal*, invited Lincoln and Mary separately to her home and encouraged them to be friends. They began courting again, meeting secretly at the Francis house, and set a wedding date of November 4. Mary Todd did not tell her sister and brother-in-law until the very morning of the wedding. The Edward's were upset, but decided if there must be a wedding, it would take place in their home. Abraham Lincoln and Mary Todd were married there that evening.

Late that night, the newlyweds moved into a four-dollar-a-week room at the Globe Tavern, a Springfield hotel that was to be their home for two years. Later that week, Lincoln ended a letter to a Shawneetown lawyer by saying, "Nothing new here, except for my marrying, which to me, is a matter of profound wonder." Their first child, named Robert Todd for Mary's father, was born on August 1, 1843.

Lincoln-Herndon Law Offices State Historic Site, Springfield, IL.

By the mid-1840s, Lincoln was making about fifteen hundred dollars a year—a good income for the time—and in January of 1844 bought a house on the corner of Eighth and Jackson Streets, a short distance from the center of town. They moved into their new home in May. A second son, Edward Baker Lincoln, was born there on March 10, 1846.

Politically, Lincoln had his eye on the Illinois Seventh Congressional District seat. He had been denied the nomination in 1843, but in May, 1846, the Whig district convention at Petersburg nominated him by acclamation. That autumn Lincoln easily defeated his Democratic opponent, a fire-and-brimstone evangelist named Peter Cartwright. After the election he returned $199.25 of $200 the Whigs had given him for campaign expenses, explaining the seventy-five cents had been spent on a barrel of hard cider for some farmers at a rally.

In October of 1847, Lincoln leased the Springfield house and set out for Washington where the Thirtieth Congress convened in December. The nation's capital was a dirty, sprawling city of some forty thousand, and the center of the south's domestic slave trade. Slaves shuffling through the streets in chains were visible from the Capitol. Saloons and gambling houses lined Pennsylvania Avenue; the city had its share of bordellos. Mrs. Lincoln stayed three months, then took the boys and went to live with her family in Lexington for the duration of her husband's congressional term.

With other Whigs in the House of Representatives, Lincoln took a strong stand against the War with Mexico and fought against expanding slavery into the territory the country acquired in the war. He stayed in the capital between terms, stumping the Northeast for General Zachary Taylor, the Whig Presidential candidate in the

1848 election. Taylor won, but Lincoln's requests for patronage jobs for Illinois politicians, a standard practice at the time, were virtually ignored. Lincoln himself was eventually offered the position of secretary of Oregon Territory, then the governorship of Oregon, but turned both down.

Disappointed with his term in Congress, Lincoln returned to Springfield in May of 1849, picking up "the practice of law with greater earnestness than ever." Then tragedy struck the house at Eighth and Jackson. In December, four-year-old Eddie Lincoln fell gravely ill (probably tuberculosis); he died on February 1, 1850. Brokenhearted, Lincoln threw himself into his work. Mary Lincoln sought solace in religion. She became pregnant, and four days before Christmas, 1850, gave birth to a son they named William Wallace. The baby, she assured Lincoln, was truly "her comfort."

In late 1850, Lincoln's father lay dying on a Coles County farm. John Johnston—Lincoln's stepbrother—wrote letters saying that Thomas would not recover and asking why Lincoln did not reply. Lincoln finally wrote Johnston in early January 1851, saying he had not responded "Because it appeared to me I could write nothing which would do any good." He sent his dying father a final message: "Tell him," he wrote Johnston, "to remember to call upon, and confide in, our great, and good, and merciful Maker: who will not turn away from him in any extremity." Thomas Lincoln died on January 15, 1851. Lincoln had not seen his father in nearly a decade; he did not attend the funeral.

The Lincoln's fourth child, named Thomas after his grandfather, was born April 4, 1853. He had a large head and wiggled like a tadpole, so they nicknamed him Tad. As he grew older, Tad had a pronounced lisp, but the impediment endeared him even more to Lincoln. Mary regarded Tad as "her little sunshine."

Eschewing politics, Lincoln concentrated on his law practice, while the slavery issue continued to draw sharp divisions across the nation, especially as new states entered the Union.

The Missouri Compromise, a series of measures passed by Congress between 1819 and 1821, allowed Missouri to enter the Union as a slave state, but banned slavery in the rest of the lands acquired by the Louisiana Purchase north of the 36° 30' line. Territories south of the line could have slavery.

But in 1854, Illinois Senator Stephen A. Douglas, Lincoln's long-time political foe, engineered the infamous Kansas-Nebraska Act. The act, which organized Kansas and Nebraska territories (both north of the 36° 30' line), provided that the slavery issue there would be settled by "popular sovereignty," the will of the people. It also declared the old Missouri Compromise "inoperative," opening to slavery the huge northern territory once reserved as a free-soil dominion.

Douglas correctly predicted the act would "raise a hell of a storm." Antislavery forces reacted violently. The Whig party, long divided over slavery, was split asunder. Democrats withdrew from the party by the thousands. Whigs, disenfranchised Democrats, abolitionists, and free-soilers held meetings in Ripon, Wisconsin, Jackson, Michigan, Washington, D.C., Ottawa and Rockford, Illinois, and formed what became the Republican Party.

Lincoln was appalled by the Kansas-Nebraska Act. To him and other northern free-soilers, the Missouri Compromise line was a sacrosanct boundary that kept slavery in check. "Thunderstruck," he ended his political hiatus and went on the stump to reelect Richard Yates, Illinois' staunch anti-Nebraska Congressman. Then, in an effort to rally the floundering Whig forces in Illinois, Lincoln and Stephen T. Logan agreed to run for the state legislature.

Douglas, meanwhile, returned to Illinois to defend his record and inspire his followers. "I could travel from Boston to Chicago by the light of my own effigy," Douglas commented. He toured the state, defending the bill. Lincoln, often speaking in the same town on the same day as Douglas, gave sharp rebuttals at Bloomington, Springfield, and Peoria.

Yates lost the November elections, but Lincoln and Logan won seats in the Illinois legislature. Lincoln, however, had his eye on the Illinois senate seat and in early 1855 resigned from the legislature to become an active candidate. At the time, U.S. Senators were elected by their respective state legislatures following the state elections. In voting at a joint session of the Illinois legislature on February 8, 1855, Lincoln led on the first five ballots, then lost to Democrat Lyman Trumbull.

As the Kansas-Nebraska Act continued to cause national tumult, Lincoln joined other anti-Nebraska leaders in calling for a state convention to gather at Bloomington in May 1856 and launch a new free-soil party in Illinois. The gathering was a coalition of old Whigs, Democrats who had bolted the party, free-soilers, and a rag-tag assortment of politicians who hated Douglas and/or the Kansas-Nebraska Act. Lincoln helped draft a party platform and draw up a slate of state Republican candidates. Called upon to give an impromptu "keynote" address, he spoke for an hour and a half, holding the crowd so spellbound that even reporters forgot to take notes. No record of the speech exists and it became known as the "Lost Speech." But partly on the strength of what Lincoln had to say that day, the Republican party was born in Illinois.

At the national Republican Convention in Philadelphia that June, John C. Fremont received the party's presidential nomination. The Illinois delegation nominated Lincoln as a favorite son candidate for Vice President, and he received 110 votes before the convention selected William Dayton, of Ohio. Lincoln was pleased, but publicly protested that he was not running for office. He campaigned hard for Fremont, making more than fifty speeches in several states, but Democrat James Buchanan won the election. Disappointed, Lincoln returned to his neglected law practice.

In 1857, the U.S. Supreme Court issued its opinion in the Dred Scott v. Sandford case. Dred Scott, a slave, sued for his freedom on the ground that his master had taken him to live temporarily in Illinois and Wisconsin Territory, where slavery was banned by the Missouri Compromise. The court ruled that blacks could not be citizens of the United States and therefore had no recourse in the Federal courts. It also declared the Missouri Compromise unconstitutional because it denied slave owners the right to take their property wherever they wanted to. The decision sent the North-South slavery controversy soaring the boiling point.

Although thoroughly enmeshed in the politics of the Scott decision and the Kansas-Nebraska Act, Lincoln, in May of 1858, traveled to Beardstown to defend Duff Armstrong, son of an old New Salem rival and friend, Jack Armstrong, on a charge of murder. Lincoln used an almanac to win the case that became part of the Lincoln legend (see Beardstown, Illinois).

That summer the Illinois Republicans saw an opportunity to put a Republican in the senate seat Stephen A. Douglas had held for more than a decade. Meeting in Springfield in June, the state convention gave Lincoln the nomination, the first time a convention had selected a senatorial candidate. Lincoln responded with his famous "House Divided" speech and again hit the campaign trail. As Douglas stumped Illinois, Lincoln followed close on his heels, often taking advantage of the crowds the Little Giant drew by speaking in the same town on the same day. In late summer and early autumn they met in a series of organized debates that gained national attention (see Lincoln-Douglas debates). It was an exhausting campaign, but when the November elections were over, Democrats outnumbered Republicans in the Illinois legislature fifty-four to forty-six, and Lincoln lost his second senatorial bid. "I feel just like the little boy who stubbed his toe," Lincoln said. "I am too big to cry and too badly hurt to laugh."

But the stage was set for 1860, when Abraham Lincoln would be the first Republican elected President of the United States.

LINCOLN HOME
NATIONAL HISTORIC SITE
Springfield, Illinois

Lincoln Home National Historic Site, Springfield, IL.

LOCATION: Corner of Eighth and Jackson Streets.

HOURS: Open daily 8:30-5; closed New Year's, Thanksgiving, and Christmas.

ADMISSION: Free. Ranger-conducted tours of the Lincoln Home are offered daily; last tour begins one-half hour before closing.

ACCESSIBILITY: The first floor of the home is wheelchair accessible. Check at the Visitor Center for information and assistance.

INFORMATION: Lincoln Home Visitor Center, 426 S. Seventh Street, Springfield, IL 62701; tel. 217-492-4241, ext. 221. www.nps.gov/liho/index.htm

The only home Abraham Lincoln owned is the centerpiece of a restored four-block area on the southeast edge of downtown Springfield. The district includes thirty-one buildings, fifteen of which date to the Lincoln era. Gas streetlights, board sidewalks, and graveled streets recreate a mid-nineteenth century Springfield neighborhood that looks much as it did in Lincoln's day.

WHAT HAPPENED HERE

The frame house at the northeast corner of Eighth and Jackson Streets was built in 1839 as a five-room, one-and-a-half story cottage. Lincoln bought the house in 1844 from the Reverend Charles Dressler, who had married the Lincolns two years earlier. He paid fifteen hundred dollars for it—twelve hundred in cash and a lot valued at three hundred dollars. There was an eighth acre of land and in the back lot were a cistern, well and pump, a privy, small barn, and a carriage house. Three blocks east the cornfields began.

The Lincolns enlarged the house several times, adding a second story in 1856 and creating an attractive Greek Revival structure.

Kitchen (original stove), Lincoln Home National Historic Site, Springfield, IL.

When at home, Lincoln curried his own horse, milked his own cow, and chopped his own firewood. But he was gone more than he was home, riding the Eighth Judicial Circuit, traveling in connection with his own political campaigns, and going on the stump for other Whig politicians. He was away so frequently that when his oldest son, Robert, was later asked for details of his father's life, Robert replied that his father wasn't home enough for him to provide much information.

Yet Lincoln loved his sons and was particularly close to the younger ones. They were frequently in his company when he was home and he was a tolerant father with little seeming concern for discipline.

With Lincoln's frequent absences, running the household and raising the children fell to Mary Lincoln. Raised in a wealthy Kentucky family that kept slaves, she was accustomed to having servants, and hired live-in help for most of the time the Lincolns lived in the house. But Mrs. Lincoln had trouble keeping servants, often complaining about the immigrant Irish girls she employed. Small matters upset her, bringing on fits of temper. She suffered violent headaches, and quarreled with tradesmen and neighbors. Often her tongue-lashings were aimed at her husband who, when he'd had enough, quietly slipped off to his office.

As with all families, there were good moments and bad in the Lincoln household. Mary Lincoln gave birth to three sons in the house at Eighth and Jackson; one died here. And it was here, in the early morning hours of November 7, 1860, that Abraham Lincoln returned from the telegraph office where he had been awaiting the election returns, to wake his sleeping wife and tell her, "Mary, we are elected."

After the election, Lincoln leased the house for $350 a year to Lucian Tilton, president of the Great Western Railroad, who commented that it looked "like the residence of a man neither rich nor poor." Lincoln never saw it again. After his death, the family continued to own it and to rent it out. Robert Todd Lincoln gave the house to the State of Illinois in 1887. It was turned over to the National Park Service in 1972 and designated a National Historic Site.

In 1988 the Lincoln home was given a badly-needed, $2.2 million restoration—enclosed in an enormous plastic bubble and, except for the plaster walls, taken completely apart and put back together. So thorough and accurate was the restoration that window panes were repaired and restored rather than replaced, and each piece of refurbished woodwork returned to its original place using the same nail holes. Some exterior clapboard beyond repair was replaced by new siding, with computer recordings made of each board so that future researchers will know exactly which pieces date to the Lincoln era. One small section of first-floor porch siding was simply repaired and repainted, leaving it intact as a museum piece.

During the restoration, original Lincoln documents popped up, literally out of the woodwork. Part of an envelope addressed and signed by Lincoln, four letters written to Lincoln, a printed anti-slavery speech, and a page from an 1855 newspaper were found in a kitchen wall. When conservators restoring the priceless furnishings at the National Park Service conservation headquarters at Harper's Ferry, West Virginia, removed the looking glass from Mr. Lincoln's shaving mirror, they found it backed with an 1844 book cover. On its reverse was a hand-penciled checker board, possibly drawn by Lincoln.

The house is now as close to the home Lincoln knew as is possible. The exterior is once again the original "Quaker Brown" color. Extensive research revealed the home's original interior to be much more colorful than previously believed, and once drab rooms are now bright and bold, decorated with swirling Victorian floral patterns. About sixty-five of more than three hundred pieces in the home have been documented as original Lincoln items, including a set of chairs, two black horsehair sofas, a pier table, and a secretary.

Park rangers conduct frequent daily guided tours, but free tickets must be obtained at the Lincoln Home Visitors Center, one block east. Tour tickets are for specific times; sometimes there is a long wait at the height of the season.

The Visitors Center offers orientation programs, films about Lincoln's time in Springfield, exhibits, and restrooms. There is a gift shop and bookstore with a good selection of publications related to Lincoln and the National Parks. Hours are the same as for the Lincoln home. Admission: Free.

While the tour system becomes overburdened at times, the Park Service, in one of the most ambitious historical restorations ever attempted, has turned Lincoln's once-drab home into a true national treasure. A visit to Springfield is not complete without seeing it.

Mr. Lincoln's Neighborhood

There were twenty-five houses along these two blocks of Eighth Street the time the Lincolns lived here; today there are twelve. These original houses provide a link to the past, to the neighborhood of the Lincoln era. Some have been restored, some are presently being restored, and some will be restored in the future.

Directly across the street is the Dean House. In 1860, the house was owned and occupied by Harriet Dean, a divorcee who was involved in teaching and gardening. Today the house contains a Lincoln exhibit entitled "What a Pleasant Home Abe Lincoln Has," which uses models, photos, and documents to trace the evolution of the Lincoln Home from the day Lincoln bought it to the day he moved out. Tours are self-guided. Admission: free.

Attorneys & Counselors at Law
★*1844-1852*

Lincoln-Herndon Law Offices State Historic Site
Springfield, Illinois

Lincoln-Herndon Law Offices State Historic Site, Springfield, IL.

Location: Corner of Sixth and Adams Streets.

Hours: Open daily 9-5 March-October, 9-4 rest of the year; last tour begins 45 minutes before closing. Closed New Year's Day, Martin Luther King, Jr. Birthday, Presidents' Day, General Election Day, Veterans Day, Thanksgiving Day, and Christmas Day.

Admission: Suggested donation.

Accessibility: Wheelchair accessible. Ask for information and assistance at the information desk.

Information: Lincoln-Herndon Law Offices State Historic Site, 209 S. Sixth Street, Springfield, IL 62701; tel. 217-785-7289. www.state.il.us/hpa/

Like many attorneys of his day, Lincoln often moved his offices. At least four different Springfield buildings in which he rented office space are known; there may have been others. However, this is the only building still standing in which Lincoln practiced law.

The red brick, Greek Revival-style building was constructed by Seth Tinsley for a store in 1840 during the building boom that followed Springfield's selection as the state capital. The first floor housed a small department store and Springfield's post office. On the second were a Federal courtroom, judges' chambers, and an office for clerks; various lawyers rented space on the third floor.

What Happened Here

Lincoln and his second law partner, Stephen Logan, moved into the building in 1843 and Lincoln kept the office when the partnership dissolved and he went into business with William Herndon a year later. It was an ideal location for an up-and-coming lawyer, with the Federal Court—the only Federal Court in Illinois between 1840 and 1848—in the same building and the state capitol, where Lincoln tried cases before the Illinois Supreme Court, located directly across the street. Nearby was the American House, Springfield's finest hotel, where Lincoln often met with visiting politicians. And the first-floor post office offered Lincoln a good place to chat with friends, neighbors, and clients for a little informal negotiating and legal "horse trading."

Herndon moved the firm to a smaller office at the rear of the building in 1847, when Lincoln left for Washington to serve his term in Congress. They kept the office when Lincoln returned in 1849 and remained there until they moved from the building in 1852.

Neither Lincoln nor Herndon were good housekeepers. The office was cluttered with worktables, a secretary with bulging drawers and overflowing pigeonholes, several heavily-laden bookcases, four or five battered, cane-bottomed chairs, and a long, rickety sofa propped against one wall. Lincoln had a habit of sprawling on the sofa and reading the morning papers aloud, distracting Herndon to the point that he often took his work into the adjoining common room that also served as the Federal Court jury room.

Nor were the two partners particularly good bookkeepers. Lincoln kept one-half of the money he received in envelopes marked with the name of the case and the words "Herndon's half," while Herndon stored the fees he collected in a small gunny sack and counted out the funds in equal shares. "Billy and I never had the scratch of a pen between us," Lincoln once said, "we just divide as we go along." Their record keeping was no better organized; Lincoln kept an envelope marked "If you can't find it anywhere else, look in here."

Above: U.S. Federal Court, Lincoln-Herndon State Historic Site, Springfield, IL.

Right: Lincoln's Law Office, Lincoln-Herndon State Historic Site, Springfield, IL.

Lincoln's last and most famous law office was located about a block away and was the office featured in *Leslies' Illustrated Weekly* in 1860, after he was elected President. It was to this office that Lincoln came on his last day in Springfield to have a final talk with Billy Herndon. They made arrangements to complete some unfinished business and Lincoln flopped down on the old sofa and began to reminisce. Finally, he gathered up an armload of books and the partners walked out to the street. Lincoln stopped and looked at the "Lincoln & Herndon" sign swinging on its rusty hinges. "Let it hang there undisturbed," he said. "Give our clients to understand that the election of a President makes no change in the firm of Lincoln and Herndon. If I live I'm coming back some time, and we'll go right on practicing law as if nothing had ever happened." The two men shook hands and Lincoln walked away. He never returned.

Guided tours of the Lincoln-Herndon law offices are offered daily. A first-floor exhibit area has displays on Lincoln's law career, including photos and copies of documents, and a short orientation video. The courtroom and offices are furnished with period pieces—law books, secretaries, quill pens, cane-bottomed chairs, wood-burning stoves. Copies of Springfield papers of the day are scattered about, as they were when Lincoln practiced law here. The offices present a realistic picture of the early stages of Lincoln's practice when his cases involved property rights, fraud, and stolen pigs. You almost expect to find a crumpled envelope marked "Herndon's half."

At the rear of the building on the lower level is a small shop called the Tinsley Dry Goods Store. Operated by the Old State Capital Foundation, it offers a variety of gifts and Lincoln memorabilia.

Old State Capitol State Historic Site

Springfield, Illinois

Old State Capitol State Historic Site, Springfield, IL.

Location: Corner of Sixth and Adams Streets.

Hours: Open daily 9-5 March-October, 9-4 rest of the year; last tour begins 45 minutes before closing. Closed New Year's Day, Martin Luther King, Jr. Birthday, Presidents' Day, General Election Day, Veterans Day, Thanksgiving Day, and Christmas Day.

Admission: Suggested donation.

Accessibility: Wheelchair accessible, enter from kiosk in Adams Street Plaza.

Information: Old State Capitol State Historic Site, Springfield, IL 62701; tel. 217-785-7960. www.state.il.us/hpa/

Abraham Lincoln was the leader of the Sangamon County legislators known as the "Long Nine" who influenced the General Assembly to move the state capital from Vandalia to Springfield (see Vandalia, Illinois). Designed by Springfield architect John F. Rague, the majestic old statehouse, with its twin, four-pillared porticos, is considered to be a near-perfect example of Greek Revival architecture, as well as one of the most historic buildings west of the Alleghenies.

The original plans called for a brick building on a stone foundation. However, when the foundation stone—a local limestone called dolomite—was quarried, its rich buff color was so attractive that it was decided to forego brick and use stone for the entire building.

What Happened Here

Although the building was not completed until 1853, some rooms and chambers were in use much earlier. From the day the statehouse opened until he left Springfield to assume the Presidency, Lincoln was an almost daily visitor. He borrowed books from the State Library and was the first person to sign out a book—a copy of revised New York laws. He frequently studied in the Law Library and tried more than two hundred cases here before the Illinois Supreme Court.

Lincoln addressed a number of political and civic meetings in the statehouse, delivering a eulogy to his political hero, Henry Clay, in the Hall of Representatives in 1852. Several of his sharpest verbal battles with his arch political rival, Stephen A. Douglas, were fought here.

1860 Lincoln-Hamlin presidential campaign poster, Old State Capitol State Historic Site, Springfield, IL.

Perhaps the most famous speech Lincoln gave here was his famed "House Divided" speech, delivered on June 16, 1858, after the delegates to the Republican State Convention endorsed him for the U.S. Senate. In part, he said:

"A house divided against itself cannot stand. I believe this Government cannot endure, permanently half slave and half free. I do not expect the Union to be dissolved—I do not expect the house to fall—but I do expect it will cease to be divided. It will become all one thing, or all the other."

The speech marked the opening salvo of Lincoln's famous debates with Douglas, which launched him into national political prominence (see Lincoln-Douglas debates).

After Lincoln received the nomination for President, he spent much time in the governor's office. Following his election in November 1860, the office became his Springfield headquarters until he left for Washington.

Stephen A. Douglas also spent much time in the statehouse and had offices here when he was Illinois Secretary of State (1840-41) and Judge of the Illinois Supreme Court (1841-43). In Washington when Confederate forces fired on Fort Sumter, Douglas hurried to the White House to offer President Lincoln his support. The two old adversaries spoke at length. Douglas released a press statement announcing his solid support for the President and the Union, then hurried home to rally Illinois Democrats to the Union cause.

On April 25, 1861, Douglas spoke before a joint session of the Illinois Legislature in the capitol. He said in part: "The first duty of an American citizen . . . is obedience to the constitution and laws of his country. I have no apprehension that any man . . . will misconstrue or misunderstand my motive . . . You all know that I am a very good partisan fighter in partisan times. And I trust you will find me equally as good a patriot when the country is in danger . . . Give me a country first, that my children may live in peace; then we will have a theatre for our party organizations to operate upon . . . I appeal to you, my countrymen—men of all parties—not to allow your passions to get the better of your judgements . . . It is with . . . a grief that I have never before experienced, that I have to contemplate this fearful struggle, but I believe in my conscience that it is a duty we owe ourselves and our children, and our God, to protect this Government and that flag from every assailant, be he who he may." It was the Little Giant's last major speech; he died in Chicago six weeks later of "acute rheumatism." He was forty-eight years old.

The Old State Capitol last saw Abraham Lincoln in death, on May 3 and 4, 1865, as his body lay in state in the House of Representative chambers. A continuous line, three deep, filed past the President's open casket for a solid twenty-four hours and thousands more were waiting when the capitol doors were closed. More than seventy-five thousand people said goodbye to Lincoln, at a time when Springfield's population was only nine thousand.

The state had outgrown its capitol building by the end of the Civil War, and construction began on a new statehouse that was completed in 1888. The Old State Capitol then became the Sangamon County Courthouse, remaining so until 1961 when it was purchased by the State of Illinois.

During the building's courthouse years, a third story was added and the interior was altered extensively. In the mid-1960s, a massive restoration program was begun. The building was completely dismantled, with each stone cataloged and stored at the state fairgrounds. The entire block was then excavated, a parking lot and offices were constructed below ground, and the Old State Capitol magnificently reconstructed to its 1840s appearance.

The first floor holds the offices of Secretary of State, Auditor of Public Accounts, State Treasurer, the State Library, Law Library, and Supreme Court Chambers, each furnished with period pieces.

On the second floor are the offices of the Adjutant General, Superintendent of Public Instruction, and Governor, committee rooms, and the Senate and House of Representatives Chambers, both furnished in exquisite detail. A huge oil painting of George Washington hangs behind the speaker's rostrum in the House chambers, another of General Lafayette decorates the Senate chambers. Both are reproductions of originals that hang in the U.S. House of Representatives. The Illinois General Assembly commissioned them in 1839, and sent James W. Berry, of Vandalia, Illinois, to Washington, D.C., to copy them.

There are some original pieces in the building, including one desk in the Senate chambers and original papers on the desks. In the anteroom of the Governor's office is one of the rails that Lincoln's cousin, John Hanks, took to the State Republican Convention in Decatur, where Lincoln received the favorite son nomination for President (see Decatur, Illinois). On a nearby wall is a huge campaign poster from 1860, touting Lincoln and his running mate, Hannibal Hamlin. A life-size marble statue of Stephen A. Douglas stands near the entrance to the House of Representatives chambers.

Right: "Mr. Lincoln's World," Old State Capitol State Historic Site, Springfield, IL.

Left: Rail that Lincoln is believed to have cut (behind rocking chair,) Old State Capitol State Historic Site, Springfield, IL.

Tours of the Old State Capitol are offered daily. "Mr. Lincoln's World," featuring special living history tours and interpreters dressed in period clothing portraying characters from the 1850s, is presented Friday and Saturday 10-noon and 1-4, except in May.

"To this place, and the kindness of these people, I owe everything."

A. Lincoln

FAREWELL TO SPRINGFIELD
★*February 11, 1961*

LINCOLN DEPOT MUSEUM

Springfield, Illinois

Lincoln Depot Museum, site of Lincoln's "Farewell Address," Springfield, IL.

LOCATION: Tenth and Monroe Streets, two blocks east of Lincoln's home.

HOURS: Open daily 10-4, April-August; closed the rest of the year.

ADMISSION: Free.

ACCESSIBILITY: Two steps to museum. Only the lower level is wheelchair accessible. Assistance is available.

INFORMATION: Tel. 217-544-8695 or 217-788-1356.

This former Great Western Railroad Depot is where Abraham Lincoln left Springfield to assume the Presidency.

What Happened Here

The impromptu farewell address Lincoln made here has been compared to the Gettysburg Address in conciseness and eloquence. Lincoln had not intended to speak that day, but as he boarded the special train that was to take him to Washington, he saw more than a thousand people standing in a cold February drizzle to bid him goodbye. He took off his hat, raised a hand for silence, and slowly said:

"My friends—No one, not in my situation, can appreciate my feelings of sadness at this parting. To this place, and the kindness of these people, I owe everything. Here I have lived a quarter of a century, and have passed from a young to an old man. Here my children have been born, and one is buried. I now leave, not knowing when, or whether ever, I may return, with a task before me greater than that which rested upon Washington. Without the assistance of the Divine Being, who ever attended him, I cannot succeed. With that assistance I cannot fail. Trusting in Him, who can go with me, and remain with you and be everywhere for good. Let us confidently hope that all will yet be well. To His care commending you, as I hope in your prayers you will commend me, I bid you an affectionate farewell."

The nineteenth-century depot has restored waiting rooms, with the gentlemen's waiting room on one side, the ladies' on the other (away from the rude language and tobacco spitting of the men). Exhibits include a diorama of Lincoln's farewell, and photos of his friends, fellow attorneys, law partners, and professional friends. A series of photos depicts the changes in Lincoln's appearance from 1846 to 1860. On the second level, a multimedia presentation depicts Lincoln's farewell and the speeches and events that took place on the journey to Washington.

Abraham Lincoln Presidential Library and Museum: Groundbreaking ceremonies for the new, $115 million dollar library and museum complex were held on Lincoln's Birthday, February 12, 2001.

The 100,000 square foot library building is scheduled to be completed in late 2002. It will house the collections of the Illinois State Historical Library, including the state's 46,000-item Lincoln collection.

Construction of the 98,000 square-foot museum will start in late 2001 and is expected to be completed in late 2004. Museum highlights include two huge exhibits covering Lincoln's childhood through his election to the Presidency and his presidential years. A "Treasury Gallery" will exhibit some of the finest pieces of the state's Lincoln collection. The museum will include theaters, a children's area, a restaurant, gift shop, and administrative offices. Located in the 200 and 300 blocks of North Sixth Street, the complex's official address will be 212 N. Sixth Street, to honor Lincoln's birthday. You can follow construction progress through a "Lincoln cam" at the Illinois Historic Preservation Agency's Presidential Library web site. www.state.il.us/hpa/preslib/default.htm

Related Lincoln Sites Downtown

Lincoln Ledger: Bank One displays the original ledger of Lincoln's account with the Springfield Marine & Fire Insurance Co. in the bank lobby. Open Monday-Friday, 9-5, closed weekends and holidays. Located at Sixth and Washington Streets on the East Old State Capitol Plaza, directly across from the Old State Capitol; tel. 217-525-9600.

First Presbyterian Church: The Lincolns began attending the First Presbyterian Church in Springfield in 1850, after the death of their son Edward. In the custom of the times, the Lincolns rented a church pew. Mrs. Lincoln became a member of the church in 1852 and, while Lincoln attended services, he was not a formal church member. That church, which was located at the corner of Third and Washington Streets, no longer stands.

The present church, built in 1868, was the site of Mary Lincoln's funeral in 1882. The old Lincoln pew is on display in the church narthex. Church tours are available Monday-Friday,

10-4 from June through September. Located at 321 S. Seventh Street, one-half block north of the Lincoln Home Visitors Center; tel. 217-528-4311. Admission: Free.

Lincoln Room, Illinois State Historical Library, Springfield, IL.

Illinois State Historical Library: The library houses a massive collection of books, manuscripts, documents, photos, paintings, and maps on Illinois history, the Civil War, and Abraham Lincoln. The Lincoln collection is considered to be second only to the Library of Congress and National Archives in the number of Lincoln documents and memorabilia; the collection of pre-presidential Lincoln documents is the largest in the world. Almost fifteen hundred original Lincoln manuscripts reside in the library vaults, including the third of five existing copies of the Gettysburg Address written entirely in Lincoln's hand; one of six existing town surveys Lincoln made during his New Salem days; the marriage license of Mary Todd and Abraham Lincoln; notes used by Lincoln in court trials and his famous debates with Stephen A. Douglas; a signed printed copy of the Emancipation Proclamation; and an autograph copy of the Thirteenth Amendment.

The library's Lincoln Room has changing displays of items in the collection, including paintings, sculptures, photographs, and documents. Unknown to many Springfield visitors, the Lincoln Room is a small gem; don't overlook it.

Located in the lower level of the Old State Capitol, the library and Lincoln Room are open Monday-Friday 8:30-5; closed Saturday, Sunday, and holidays. Admission: Free. Additional information: Illinois State Historical Library, Old State Capitol, Springfield, IL 62701; tel. 217-524-7216. www.state.il.us/hpa/lib/

Site of Globe Tavern, Springfield, IL.

GLOBE TAVERN: The inn where Abraham and Mary Todd Lincoln first set up housekeeping stood on Adams Street between Third Street and Fourth Street. The site is marked by a bronze plaque atop a concrete pillar, which stands beneath a Sycamore tree at the front of a parking lot. The inscription on the plaque reads: " On this site stood the Globe Tavern, the home of Abraham Lincoln and his wife from the time of their marriage on November 4, 1842 until May 2, 1844. Here their first child was born."

The Final Resting Place
★*1865*

Lincoln's Tomb State Historic Site
Springfield, Illinois

Lincoln's Tomb State Historic Site, Springfield, IL.

Location: Oak Ridge Cemetery.

Hours: Open daily 9-5 March-October, daily 9-4 rest of the year; closed New Year's Day, Martin Luther King, Jr. Birthday, Presidents' Day, General Election Day, Veterans Day, Thanksgiving Day, and Christmas Day.

Admission: Free.

Accessibility: Wheelchair accessible, smooth walkways. Upper level not wheelchair accessible.

Information: Lincoln's Tomb State Historic Site, Oak Ridge Cemetery, Springfield, IL 62702; tel. 217-782-2717. www.state.il.us/hpa/

Getting There: The cemetery is two miles north of downtown. Travel north on Sixth Street to N. Grand Avenue, turn left and go two blocks to the cemetery entrance. The route is marked with signs.

The most impressive of Springfield's many Lincoln memorials is the slain President's tomb. Designed by Vermont sculptor Larken Mead, the imposing monument dominates a six-acre plot in Oak Ridge Cemetery.

Larken Mead statue of Lincoln, Lincoln's Tomb State Historic Site, Springfield, IL.

What Happened Here

The controversy that swirled around Lincoln's Presidency followed him in death. Soon after Lincoln's murder, a Springfield committee was formed to make arrangements for his interment until an appropriate shrine could be built. Hurried construction of a temporary vault began and, by working day and night, the structure was nearly ready when Lincoln's body arrived in Springfield on May 3—eighteen days after his assassination.

Then the battle began. Mrs. Lincoln refused to use the vault, even temporarily, demanding that Lincoln be interred in Oak Ridge Cemetery. On May 4, the bodies of her husband and of her son William, who died in Washington in 1862, were placed in the cemetery's public receiving vault.

The committee, believing that Mrs. Lincoln would change her mind, completed the vault. But she remained adamant, threatening to return Lincoln's body to Washington, D.C., and there was little to do but tear down the $50,000 sepulchre.

There still remained the problem of where to inter Lincoln's remains until a memorial could be built. The public receiving vault at Oak Ridge, the only one in the cemetery, could not be closed for an indefinite period. So, with much ill feeling toward Mrs. Lincoln, an exact duplicate of the committee's original vault (it had stood on the site of the present State Capitol) was built at Oak Ridge. In December, 1871, Lincoln's body, along with those of his sons William and Edward (the second-born who died in Springfield in 1850), were placed there.

Ground was broken for the permanent memorial in 1869. By July, 1871, when Thomas (Tad) Lincoln died in Chicago, the catacomb section was ready for use and Lincoln and his sons were placed in a crypt in the uncompleted memorial. But first, Lincoln's casket was opened and thirteen members of what had become the National Lincoln Monument Association viewed the corpse and signed papers testifying that it was Lincoln. The memorial was dedicated on October 15, 1874, in ceremonies attended by President Ulysses S. Grant. Members of the Monument Association again viewed Lincoln's body and verified the identity. The casket was then placed in a marble sarcophagus in the center of the burial chamber, which could be seen from the outside through a small window.

Following an attempt to steal Lincoln's body in 1876, the coffin was secretly removed from the sarcophagus and hidden deep within the recesses of the tomb. Only the custodian and a select few knew the exact location and, until 1899, those who came to pay homage to Lincoln gazed unknowingly at an empty sarcophagus. In 1887, the bodies of Lincoln and his wife, who died in 1882, were secretly placed in a brick vault below the floor of the burial chamber.

By 1899, the memorial was badly deteriorated and required complete rebuilding. Once again Lincoln's body was moved and, along with those of his family, secretly interred in an underground mausoleum at Oak Ridge.

When the memorial's restoration was completed in 1901, the bodies of Mrs. Lincoln, William, Edward, and Thomas were placed in crypts in the wall. At Robert Lincoln's direction, Lincoln was interred beneath the floor of the burial chamber, in a concrete and steel vault covered with twenty inches of concrete. But first, the casket was opened for a third, and final, time. Twenty-two men who had known him in Springfield were present, and each attested that the body was that of Abraham Lincoln. Then, at long last, the President was laid to his final rest.

The monument was rebuilt again in 1930, when interior passages were added to provide public access to the burial chamber.

An obelisk rising 117 feet into the air tops the memorial. A second level terrace, reached by broad granite steps at each corner, holds large statues of Civil War fighting forces—the Infantry, Cavalry, Artillery, and Navy—all the work of Larken Mead, as is the statue of Lincoln on the face of the obelisk. Cemented into the obelisk is a Roman stone dating from 578 BC, a gift of the people of Rome at the time of Lincoln's death.

At the memorial entrance is a large bronze head of Lincoln by the sculptor Gutzon Borglum, the nose polished bright by the touch of millions of hands. You are invited to touch—legend says it brings good luck. Inside, statuettes of Lincoln by Daniel Chester French, Leonard Crunelle, Fred M. Torrey, Augustus Saint-Gaudens, Aldoph A. Weinman, and Lorado Taft line the marble corridors leading to the burial chamber. Here, too, are bronze plaques inscribed with Lincoln's Farewell Address, the Gettysburg Address, a portion of the Second Inaugural Address, and a biography of Lincoln.

In the solemn burial chamber, a seven-ton block of red granite inscribed, "Abraham Lincoln 1809-1865" marks Lincoln's final resting place—thirty inches behind the marker and ten feet below the surface of the floor. The flags of seven states significant in Lincoln's life—Massachusetts, New Jersey, Pennsylvania, Virginia, Kentucky, Indiana, and Illinois—along with the National colors and the presidential emblem, circle the marker. Inscribed on the wall above are the words spoken by Secretary of War Edwin M. Stanton at the moment of Lincoln's death:

"Now He Belongs to the Ages."

Lincoln's final resting place, Springfield, IL.

The 114th Regiment drill ceremony, Lincoln's Tomb, Springfield, IL.

Each Tuesday evening, June through August, the 114th Infantry Regiment—a reactivated Civil War unit dressed in authentic uniforms—conducts a retreat ceremony at the memorial. Muskets and a mortar are fired before the flag is lowered, folded, and presented to a spectator selected at random. Highly-moving, the ceremony is well worth arranging your schedule to see—be sure to sign the guest register in advance. Additional information: tel. 217-782-2717.

Special services and pilgrimages by veterans organizations are conducted at Lincoln's Tomb on and near Lincoln's birthday in February.

Elsewhere in Oak Ridge Cemetery are the graves of labor leader John L. Lewis, the famous Illinois poet Vachel Lindsay,

Lincoln's law partner, William Herndon, and four Illinois governors. Also to be seen are the receiving vault in which Lincoln was originally buried, the poignant Illinois Vietnam Veterans Memorial, and the Illinois Korean War Memorial.

William Herndon grave site, Oak Ridge Cemetery, Springfield, IL.

Elsewhere in and around Downtown

Capitol Complex Visitors Center: The center has exhibits, a video, and information about the Capitol complex, including the State Capitol, the State Archives, State Library and state office buildings, along with information about sites and attractions throughout Illinois. Located at 425 S. College (enter on Edwards Street between College and Pasfield), the center is open Monday-Friday 8-4:30, Saturday-Sunday 9-4; closed Sunday and holidays. Admission: Free. Additional information: tel. 217-524-6620.

Illinois State Capitol: While the first legislative session was held in the new capitol in 1887, the building is still known as the New State Capitol. The central building in the Capitol Complex, it houses the Illinois state legislative and constitutional offices. Its grounds extend three blocks along Second Street and features numerous statues and sculptures. The statue, "Abraham Lincoln," by the sculptor Leonard Volk, stands before the capitol at Second Street. At 361 feet, the capitol dome is seventy-four feet taller than the U.S. Capitol dome and one of the tallest buildings in central Illinois. Inside the dome are a stained-glass skylight bearing the State Seal of Illinois, murals, and a bas-relief frieze. Murals and other works of art are found throughout the building. A gift shop offers books, souvenirs, and specialty items.

Free guided tours are given 9-3, on the hour and half hour weekdays, hourly on Saturday. Located at Second Street and Capitol, the building is open Monday-Friday 8-4, Saturday-Sunday 9-3; closed New Year's Day, Easter, Thanksgiving Day and day after, Christmas Eve Day and Christmas Day. Admission: Free. Additional information: tel. 217-782-2099

Illinois State Museum: Also part of the Capitol Complex, the museum has three floors of exhibits on Illinois history, natural history, anthropology, and art. "A Place for Discovery" features a hands-on exhibit area for children (closed Mondays), and the state-of-the-art, computer-interactive exhibit, "At Home in the Heartland," allows visitors to participate in real-life scenarios of Illinois residents from the 1700s through the 1970s. The "Peoples of the Past" exhibit features realistic life-size dioramas of Illinois' Native American heritage, while galleries highlight

Top Right: Illinois State Capitol, Springfield, IL. Lincoln statue by Leonard W. Volk.

Top Left: Leonard W. Volk statue of Lincoln, Illinois State Capitol, Springfield, IL.

Bottom Left: Statue of Steven A. Douglas, grounds of the Illinois State Capitol, Springfield, IL.

photography, and fine and decorative arts. Audiophones explain exhibits. Special events include guided tours, lectures, films, and field study trips; light snacks are available at Cafe Musee except during winter. The museum shop offers books, souvenirs, and specialty gift items. Located at Spring and Edwards Streets, the museum is open Monday-Saturday 8:30-5, Sunday noon-5; closed New Year's Day, Easter Sunday, Thanksgiving Day, and Christmas Day. Admission: Free. Additional information: tel. 217-782-7386. www.museum.state.il.us/

Executive Mansion: This huge Victorian home, the third-oldest continuously occupied governor's mansion in the nation, contains many beautiful antiques and historic artifacts. Seven U.S. presidents, including Abraham Lincoln, have been received here. Rooms on three levels are open to the public including four formal parlors; a state dining room; four bedrooms, including the Lincoln bedroom; and a library crafted from Black Walnut. The mansion's Lincoln artifacts include portraits of the Lincolns and their close friend Edward Baker, china from the Lincoln White House, a bust of Lincoln modeled from life by Thomas Jones, and a table presented to President Lincoln. The Executive Mansion is located close to downtown at 410 E. Jackson Street, with guided tours given Tuesday and Thursday, 9:30-11 and 2-3:30, Saturday 9:30-11. Closed New Year's Day, Martin Luther King, Jr. Birthday, Lincoln's Birthday, President's Day, Memorial Day, Independence Day, Labor Day, Columbus Day, Thanksgiving and the day after, and Christmas Day. Admission: Free. Additional information: tel. 217-782-6450.

Dana-Thomas House State Historic Site: Designed by famed architect Frank Lloyd Wright, the house was built in 1902 for Springfield socialite Susan Lawrence Dana. Considered to be one of the most complete of Wright's early Prairie-style designs, it contains the largest collection of original Wright-designed furniture and art glass of any of the architect's structures. Wright designed many built-ins and about one hundred free-standing pieces of furniture. A stunning collection of art glass includes 450 windows, light fixtures, skylights, and door panels. Guided tours of the magnificently-restored home begin in the Visitor Center, which is a Wright-designed carriage house, and include a slide show/orientation program. A gift shop offers books and specialty items. Located at 301 E. Lawrence Avenue, the home is open Wednesday-Sunday 9-4 (last tour begins at 4 P.M.); closed New Year's Day, Martin Luther King, Jr. Birthday, Presidents Day, General Election Day, Veteran's Day, Thanksgiving Day, and Christmas Day. Admission: Suggested donation. Additional information: tel. 217-782-6776. www.state.il.us/hpa/

VACHEL LINDSAY HOME: The international poet (1879-1931) known as the "Prairie Troubadour" wrote many works about Lincoln, including the haunting "Abraham Lincoln Walks at Midnight." The home contains original fixtures, furnishings, artwork, and works by Lindsay. Once owned by Abraham Lincoln's sister-in-law, it was the site of Lincoln's pre-inaugural farewell reception and is a national historic landmark. Located at 603 S. Fifth Street, the restored home is open to visitors. Additional information: tel. 217-524-0901 or 217-785-7290. www.state.il.us/hpa/

ELSEWHERE IN SPRINGFIELD

EDWARDS PLACE: Built in 1833, this beautifully-preserved mansion is the oldest house on its own grounds in Springfield and was the center of the city's social and political life for many years. The nineteenth-century-style furnishings include sculpture, paintings, porcelains, and Indian objects. Also home to the Springfield Art Association, which now extends to an adjoining complex housing the Michael Victor II Art Library, galleries, and an art school. Located at 700 N. Fourth Street, gallery hours are Monday-Friday 9-5, Saturday 10-3. Historic home tours are by appointment only and require several days advance notice. Admission: Suggested donation. Additional information: tel. 217-523-2631.

GRAND ARMY OF THE REPUBLIC MEMORIAL MUSEUM:
This small museum offers a wealth of Civil War memorabilia, including a 35-star flag taken from Ford's Theater in Washington on April 15, 1865, the night Lincoln was assassinated and

bunting used during a Lincoln tour in Illinois. There are Civil War weapons and equipment, along with tintypes by Civil War photographer Matthew Brady, donated to the National Women's Relief Corps in tribute to the Union veterans of the War Between the States. Located at 629 S. Seventh Street, open 10-4, Tuesday-Saturday, closed Memorial Day, Independence Day, Labor Day, Veterans Day, Thanksgiving Day, Christmas Eve Day and Christmas Day. Admission: Free; tel. 217-522-4373.

Washington Park Botanical Gardens: The gardens include a domed conservatory, perennial scent and texture gardens, various floral display areas, and a formal rose garden, which is best seen in mid-June. Six indoor flower shows are held each year. The outdoor gardens may be seen anytime; the conservatory is open Monday through Friday noon-4, Saturday and Sunday noon-5; closed Christmas Eve Day and Christmas Day. Admission: Free. Located at 1740 W. Fayette Street, Washington Park. Additional information: tel. 217-753-6228.

Thomas Reese Memorial Carillon: Located in Washington Park, adjacent to the botanical gardens, this magnificent carillon is the fifth largest in the world and one of the few open to visitors. Three observation decks in the twelve-story tower permit close inspection of sixty-six imported bells. Tours are offered Tuesday and Sunday noon to 8, June through August; Saturday and Sunday noon to sunset, late spring and early autumn. Admission: Adults $2; students $1.50. Additional information: Tel. 217-544-1751 or 217-753-6219.

Henson Robinson Zoo: The zoo is home to more than 33 species of exotic animals and native animals, including endangered species, some of which are involved in a global program to ensure the survival of endangered and threatened species. The zoo's lemur exhibit is one of only three collections in the country. Zoo facilities include a petting area, gift shop, and concessions. Located at 1100 East Lake Drive, the zoo is open Monday-Friday 10-5, Saturday and Sunday 10-6, late March to mid-October; closed the rest of the year. Admission: Adults $2.50; age 62 and up, and ages 3-12, $1.50. Additional information: tel. 217-753-6217.

Springfield Area

Camp Butler National Cemetery: This impressive National Cemetery, established in 1862 on the grounds of a Union Civil War training center and Confederate prison, contains of the remains of thousands of Civil War troops, including 837 Confederate soldiers. Here, too, are buried the dead of other wars—the Spanish-American War, World War I, World War II, Korea, and Vietnam, including thirty-five foreign prisoners of war from World War II and Korea. Located six miles northeast of Springfield on U.S. Highway 36 at 5063 Camp Butler Road, the cemetery is open daily 8-dusk. Additional information: tel. 217-492-4070.

Nearby Accommodations:
Renaissance Springfield Hotel (316 rooms), 701 E. Adams Street, Springfield, IL 62701; tel. 800-HOTELS-1 or 217-544-8800.

Drury Inn and Suites (118 rooms), 3180 S. Dirksen Parkway, Springfield, IL 62703, tel. 800-325-8300 or 217-529-3900. www.druryinn.com

The Inn at 835 offers bed and breakfast accommodations in a National Historic Landmark built in 1909. Located at 835 S. 2nd. Street, Springfield, IL 62704; tel. 888-217-4835 or 217-523-4466. www.innat835.com/

Maldaner's Restaurant, 222 S. Sixth Street, tel. 217-522-4313.

Mountain Jack's Steakhouse, 2830 Stephenson Dr., tel. 217-529-6623.

Norb Andy's, 518 E. Capitol, tel. 523-7777.

Additional Information:
Springfield Convention and Visitors Bureau, 109 N. Seventh Street, Springfield, IL 62701. Open 8-5, Monday-Friday; tel. 800-545-7300 or 217-789-2360. www.visit-springfieldillinois.com/

"NO HUMAN BEING WOULD ENDURE WHAT WE USED TO ON THE CIRCUIT. I HAVE SLEPT WITH TWENTY MEN IN THE SAME ROOM—SOME ON BED ROPES—SOME ON QUILTS—SOME ON SHEETS, A STRAW OR TWO UNDER THEM. AND OH—SUCH VICTUALS—GOOD GOD!"

(LINCOLN'S LAW PARTNER)

EIGHTH JUDICIAL CIRCUIT

Because of relatively small populations in the early and mid-nineteenth century, most Illinois counties could not support a full time judge. Illinois' circuit court system, adopted in 1839, divided the state into multi-county circuits, each with a judge who traveled from county to county, holding court and conducting the judicial business of the county.

The attorneys of the day served the same thinly-scattered population. Many, including Abraham Lincoln, had to follow the circuit in order to make a living. These circuit-riding lawyers met with their clients on courthouse lawns, under nearby trees, or on the public streets. At night they gathered in the village inns, eating and drinking together, often sharing a common bedroom with the judge and, occasionally, defendants and plaintiffs in a case.

It was a hard life, with small fees, often primitive living conditions, and extensive, difficult travel. In the early days it was known as the Mud Circuit.

The Eighth Judicial Circuit at its peak included an area of some ten thousand square miles (about the size of Maryland) covering a fifth of the entire state. The boundaries changed from time to time, and county seats were often moved, but from 1843 to 1853 it was made up of fourteen counties. The judge and lawyers always visited in the same order: Sangamon, Tazewell, Woodford, McLean, Logan, DeWitt, Piatt, Champaign, Vermilion, Edgar, Shelby, Moultrie, Macon, and Christian. The judge and lawyers were on the road some three months at a time, traveling by horse or buggy and stopping at the county seats for court terms of two days to several weeks.

Most lawyers cared little for the life, but Lincoln seemed to thrive in the environment. He rode the circuit full-time for more than a dozen years, and part-time for several more, making the four hundred-mile journey twice a year, beginning in March and September. His famous storytelling sessions, the friendships he formed, and the political contacts he made apparently compensated for the months of travel. Except for the two years he served in Congress, Lincoln traveled the circuit until he was elected President.

If the county seats were nearby, Lincoln sometimes returned to Springfield on weekends. After 1857, he could reach every circuit town by train. The improvements in transportation, along with a reduction in the size of the district, made the life on the circuit somewhat less difficult in later years.

On the circuit, when they could not make a court appearance, it was not uncommon for judges to designate attorneys as judges. Judge David Davis, of Bloomington, often called on Lincoln to take the bench when he was away and Lincoln was highly regarded, even by other attorneys, for his wisdom and fair judgement.

All the important covenants of county life and land were performed at the courthouses. The first were built of logs or were wood frame structures. But after 1840, courthouses became elaborate affairs, usually constructed of brick, and often sporting columned porticos and soaring cupolas. A courthouse was, in many cases, the county seat's finest building.

Two original courthouses, along with one reproduction, remain in Lincoln's old Eighth Judicial Circuit.

POSTVILLE COURTHOUSE STATE HISTORIC SITE
Lincoln, Illinois

Postville Courthouse State Historic site, Lincoln, IL.

LOCATION: 914 Fifth Street; Logan County.

HOURS: Open Tuesday-Saturday, noon-5; closed New Year's Day,
Martin Luther King, Jr. Birthday, Presidents' Day, Veterans Day, General Election Day, Thanksgiving, and Christmas.

ADMISSION: Suggested donation.

ACCESSIBILITY: Two steps to courthouse; upper level not wheelchair accessible.

INFORMATION: Postville Courthouse State Historic Site, P.O. Box 355, Lincoln, IL 62656; tel. 217-732-8930. www.state.il.us/hpa/

GETTING THERE: Lincoln is 31 miles northeast of Springfield, 31 miles southwest of Bloomington via I-55. To reach the courthouse from I-55, take Exit 126 (Route 10), at first stoplight turn south, travel south to next stoplight (Fifth

Street), turn east and go five blocks to the courthouse.

The old Postville Courthouse still stands, but not in Lincoln. After 1847 the building was no longer used as a courthouse and was eventually remodeled into private housing. By the early twentieth century, it was a mere shadow of its former self. In 1929 Henry Ford, wresting historic buildings and entire farms from the land for his new Greenfield Village Museum, purchased the courthouse where Lincoln had practiced law. It was torn down, board by board and nail by nail, shipped to Dearborn, Michigan, and reconstructed in the historical village. It still stands in Dearborn, facing the village green, adjacent to the Thomas Edison laboratories.

The present Postville Courthouse is a reproduction, built in the 1950s with plans drawn from the original in Dearborn. It houses an exhibit area and an 1840s-style courtroom.

What Happened Here

Founded in 1835, the village of Postville became the seat of newly-created Logan County in 1837, defeating Mt. Pulaski for the honor by one vote, mainly because town developers offered to construct a new courthouse at no cost to the county. The two-story, walnut-sided building was erected at a cost of $1,176.83. County offices occupied the first floor, with a small courtroom on the second level. Adjacent to it, the county added a two-story, twelve-foot-square log jail paneled inside with oak planks two inches thick. While the courthouse was under construction, court sessions were held in the dining room of Dr. John Deskins' Tavern across the street.

Postville Courthouse was also a civic center and meeting hall, and was even used as a church. But the high points of its calendar were invariably the semiannual "Court Weeks," which always brought a holiday air to towns on the circuit. As one traveler wrote: "Not only suitors, jurors and witnesses, but all who can spare the time, brush up their coats and brush down their horses to go to court."

The Logan County seat was moved to Mt. Pulaski in 1847, for much the same reason it was originally established in Postville—Mt. Pulaski officials erected a fine new courthouse.

A fire in 1857 destroyed Logan County's records, so little is known about the cases Lincoln handled at Postville. Once, when Lincoln was absent from a court session, Judge Treat sent the sheriff, Dr. Deskins, to find him. Deskins finally found Lincoln in Postville Park, "playing townball with the boys."

After Mt. Pulaski became the Logan County seat, the Postville courthouse was sold at auction to a local resident for three hundred dollars. It continued to be used for civic and religious purposes for a time, but by 1880 had been remodeled into a private home, remaining so until Henry Ford bought the building.

The main floor of the newly-refurbished Postville Courthouse has an exhibit area introducing the Eighth Judicial Circuit and offers changing displays on Lincoln and area history. While no record exists of how Postville's courtroom actually looked, the second level has a small courtroom with period furnishings—a judge's bench, attorneys' tables, jury chairs. There are original documents pertaining to the times, but not to Lincoln. Several special events are held each year at the Postville Courthouse.

Site where Lincoln christened the community of Lincoln, Illinois, with watermelon juice.

Lincoln, Illinois (pop. 15,400)

Lincoln is the first community in the United States named after Abraham Lincoln and was so christened by Lincoln himself. Developers of the town used Lincoln's services to prepare the necessary legal documents to sell lots and decided to name it in his honor. On August 27, 1853, the day the first lots were sold,

Lincoln broke open a watermelon and christened his namesake with its juice. The spot was near the present Amtrak railway station, at the corner of Sangamon and Broadway Streets. Lincoln became the Logan County seat in 1855 and absorbed the old village of Postville into its municipal boundaries in 1865.

A brochure outlining a walking tour of historic downtown Lincoln is available at the Abraham Lincoln Tourism Bureau of Logan County, 303 S. Kickapoo Street.

A number of historical markers indicate important Abraham Lincoln sites in the city, although the original buildings no longer stand.

Historical Markers

Robert B. Latham Home, corner of Delavan and Kickapoo Streets. "On this site stood the home of Robert B. Latham who joined John D. Gillette and Virgil Hickox to found the town of Lincoln in 1853. Abraham Lincoln, judges, and lawyers of the Eighth Judicial Circuit were frequent guests at his home."

Postville Park, corner of Fifth and Washington Streets. "In 1835 Russell Post, a Baltimore adventurer, laid out the town of Postville which became the first Logan County seat. The town square is now Postville Park. Here Abraham Lincoln and his friends played townball, a predecessor of baseball, threw the mall, a heavy wooden hammer, and pitched horseshoes."

Deskins Tavern, corner of Fifth and Madison Streets. "On this site Dr. John Deskins erected a tavern in 1836. Abraham Lincoln, David Davis and other lawyers frequently stayed overnight here while the Eighth Judicial Circuit Court was in session at the Postville Courthouse. The judge, lawyers, litigants, witnesses, jurors and prisoners often shared the same dinner table."

Stephen A. Douglas speech, corner of Decatur and Sangamon Streets. "On this site during the senatorial campaign of 1858, Stephen A. Douglas spoke to a Democratic political rally in a circus tent on September 4th. Douglas' opponent for the senate seat, Abraham Lincoln, was on the train from Bloomington to Springfield and stopped to hear the speech."

LINCOLN HOUSE, 501 Broadway Street. "On this site the town proprietors erected the original Lincoln House in 1854. Leonard Volk met Abraham Lincoln on the sidewalk in front of the hotel on July 16, 1858, and arranged to make Lincoln's life mask later."

ABRAHAM LINCOLN AND LINCOLN, ILLINOIS, corner of Broadway and Sangamon Streets. "Near this site Abraham Lincoln christened the town with the juice of a watermelon when the first lots were sold on August 27, 1853. President-elect Lincoln spoke here, November 21, 1860, while traveling to Chicago and Lincoln's funeral train stopped here, May 3, 1865, before completing the trip to Springfield."

OTHER LINCOLN ATTRACTIONS

LOGAN COUNTY COURTHOUSE: Erected in 1905, this attractive Greek Revival courthouse is the third constructed here since 1853. Lincoln practiced law in two previous courthouses that stood here and during the March term in 1859, substituted for Judge David Davis as the presiding judge of the Logan County Circuit Court.

The present stone courthouse has a magnificent dome with four large clocks, stained-glass insets, and a cupola. A statue of Lincoln stands in the first floor rotunda. Local history exhibits are displayed in some hallways. On the third floor balcony under the dome are large murals of the Postville Courthouse, Mt. Pulaski Courthouse, the community of Lincoln, and portraits of Lincoln and other notables of his time. Take a few moments to browse here, for the dome and Lincoln murals are typical out-of-the-way treasures usually discovered by accident. Located at the corner of Pulaski and McLean Streets, the courthouse is open Monday-Friday 8-5; closed Saturday, Sunday, and holidays. Admission: Free. Additional information:
tel. 217-732-8687.

Lincoln College: Ground-breaking ceremonies for Lincoln University, now Lincoln College, were held on Lincoln's birthday, February 12, 1865. The massive, Italinate University Hall, the first campus building, is listed on the National Register of Historic Places and still serves Lincoln College students.

"Lincoln the Student," by Merrill Gage, Lincoln College Campus, Lincoln, Il.

At McKinstry Memorial Library, on Keokuk Street, is the statue "Lincoln the Student," by the sculptor Merrill Gage, depicting a seated Lincoln reading a book. The library houses two little-known museums that are true treasures. The Museum of Presidents honors the nation's Chief Executives from George Washington through the present. There is a photograph of each President (paintings or other artwork of those who served before the camera was invented), a brief biography of each, and documents bearing each President's signature. In all but a few cases, there are documents signed by each First Lady, as well. Located in the library lobby, it's a strong and impressive collection.

In an adjoining room, the comfortable Lincoln Museum (thick carpets ease weary feet) displays an outstanding collection of Lincoln material. Dioramas depict Lincoln at the Postville Courthouse, Lincoln christening the community with watermelon juice, Lincoln as a surveyor, and the President's funeral train stopping in Lincoln.

The collection includes several thousand Lincoln artifacts. The highlights of items used by Lincoln, his family, or associates include: A coal oil lamp and china from the Lincoln home in Springfield; a rocking chair and table that belonged to Thomas (Tad) Lincoln; a desk Lincoln used while serving in the Illinois legislature; a chair from the Lincoln White House; law books used by Lincoln and William Herndon; and a table once owned by Mentor Graham, who helped Lincoln with his studies of grammar and mathematics in New Salem.

Left: Table once owned by Mentor Graham, of New Salem, Lincoln College Museum, Lincoln, IL.
Right: Rocking chair that once belonged to Thomas "Tad" Lincoln, Lincoln College Museum, Lincoln, IL.

Counter-style glass cases display many articles that belonged to Mary Lincoln—personal letters, jewelry, a fan, handkerchiefs, scissors she used in Springfield, and a lock of her hair. There are numerous items from Lincoln's 1860 presidential campaign, documents bearing his signature, and paintings, busts, and statuettes of Lincoln, including the life mask and hands of Lincoln by Chicago sculptor Leonard Volk. Volk, whose wife was a cousin of Stephen A. Douglas, made arrangements to do the work when he met Lincoln on the street here in Lincoln. The castings were made at Volk's Chicago studio in March 1860 and are perhaps his best known work.

A display of items pertaining to Lincoln's assassination includes tassels from the casket and catafalque covering used when Lincoln's body lay in state at the Old State Capitol in Springfield. There is a piece of the dress worn by the actress

Laura Keene, who was starring in Our American Cousin at Ford's Theatre in Washington the night Lincoln was shot. The dress was stained with Lincoln's blood when the actress cradled Lincoln's head in her lap. Among other items are a lock of Lincoln's hair, clipped from his head at the tomb, a derringer pistol of the type with which he was murdered, and examples of "Mourning Drape," a pattern glass created after Lincoln's death.

Desk used by Lincoln while serving in the Illinois General Assembly, Springfield; Lincoln College Museum, Lincoln, IL.

The collection includes many documents bearing Lincoln's signature, an 1860 campaign poster that was reproduced in *Leslie's Illustrated*, and a copy of the *Illinois Journal* of April 20, 1848, featuring a small ad for "Lincoln & Herndon—Attorneys & Counselors at Law."

The museum has thousands of artifacts in its vaults, many of which are rotated in and out of the exhibits.

The Lincoln Museum is located at 300 Keokuk Street and is open Monday-Friday 9-4, Saturday and Sunday 1-4; closed holidays and mid-December-February 1. Admission: Free. Additional information: Tel. 217-732-3155.

NATIONAL RAILSPLITTING FESTIVAL: Held the second weekend after Labor Day, the festival features rail-splitting contests, arts and crafts shows, food, and name entertainment.

Nearby Accommodations:
Holiday Inn Express (70 rooms), 130 Olson Road, Lincoln, IL 62656; tel. 217-735-5800.

Super 8 Motel (45 rooms), 2800 Woodlawn Road, Lincoln, IL 62656; tel. 217-732-8886.

Blue Dog Inn, 111 S. Sangamon Street, tel. 217-735-1743.

Guzzardo's Italian Villa, 509 Pulaski Street, tel. 217-732-6370.

Additional Information:
Abraham Lincoln Tourism Bureau
of Logan County, 303 Kickapoo, Lincoln, IL 62656;
tel. 217-732-8687. www.logancountytourism.org/

MT. PULASKI COURTHOUSE STATE HISTORIC SITE

Mt. Pulaski, Illinois

Mt. Pulaski Courthouse State Historic Site, Mt. Pulaski, IL.

LOCATION: Town Square; Logan County.

HOURS: Open Tuesday-Saturday 12-5 March-October, Tuesday-Saturday 12-4 rest of the year; closed New Year's Day, Martin Luther King, Jr. Birthday, Presidents' Day, Veterans Day, General Election Day, Thanksgiving, and Christmas.

ADMISSION: Free.

ACCESSIBILITY: Not wheelchair accessible.

INFORMATION: Mt. Pulaski Courthouse State Historic Site, City Square, Mt. Pulaski, IL 62548; tel. 217-792-3919 or 217-732-8930. www.state.il.us/hpa/

GETTING THERE: Mt. Pulaski is 11 miles southeast of Lincoln on Route 121. Turn east at historical marker at DeKalb Street, travel four blocks to Vine Street, turn south two blocks to Jefferson, turn east and travel two blocks to City Square.

Dominating the center of a town square lined with nineteenth-century brick buildings, the Mt. Pulaski Courthouse saw much of Lincoln during the seven years the town served as the county seat. Mt. Pulaski became the Logan County seat in 1847, winning the honor much as Postville had—by offering a fine new courthouse and, in this case, a booming business block. Local citizens, craftsmen, and merchants donated materials and labor and raised $2,700 to construct the building.

WHAT HAPPENED HERE

One of only two surviving Illinois courthouses of the original fourteen that were part of the Eighth Judicial Circuit, Mt. Pulaski Courthouse is the only one that is restored, furnished, and interpreted as an operating 1850s courthouse. It is listed on the National Register of Historic Places. Unfortunately, the details of Lincoln's legal career at Mt. Pulaski have been lost to history, consumed in the 1857 fire that destroyed Logan County's records.

But one trial that took place here—known as the "horological cradle" case—lives on as part of the Lincoln legend. The case involved a man who had traded some land for a patent on a "clockwork" baby cradle, then changed his mind and sued to get his land back. In court, Lincoln described the patent as "a cradle, rocked by machinery, with weights running on pulleys, the cradle was the pendulum and which being wound up would rock itself until it ran down, thus saving time to mothers and nurses." Lincoln then set the machine in motion. After it ran for a time, Judge David Davis asked how it could be shut off. Lincoln replied, "It's like some of the glib talkers you and I know, Judge, it won't stop until it runs down." The man got his land back.

Mt. Pulaski's heyday was short-lived. Set at the far southeastern corner of the county, it was a poor location for a county seat. But the main blow came in 1852 when the first railroad in the county passed far from the town. Lincoln, however, had been founded next to the new railroad and the economic and population boom the rail line brought completely overshadowed Mt. Pulaski. Lincoln became the new Logan County seat in 1855.

Over the years the former courthouse was used as a school, city offices, library, and post office. Mt. Pulaski firemen held meetings and dances in the second level courtroom, and the local American

Legion post met here. In 1936 the town deeded the building to the state to be used as a museum.

Restored courtroom, Mt. Pulaski Courthouse State Historic Site, Mt. Pulaski, IL.

The brick, two-story Greek Revival courthouse has been restored to its appearance in Lincoln's day. Surrounded by stately oaks and maples, it dominates the town square, reinforcing the importance of courthouses in the mid-nineteenth century, when they were called "county capitols." The lower level has the offices of county officials of the day—the county surveyor, treasurer, sheriff, clerk of circuit court, and county court clerk—restored with period pieces, although none are original. A jail in the basement has not been restored.

The second level courtroom is beautiful restoration, projecting the image that important things happened here. Conservators removing the floor during restoration found the original floor underneath, intact right down to the holes for the spindles used in the judge's stand.

Attorney's table, Mt. Pulaski Courthouse State Historic Site, Mt. Pulaski, IL.

The raised judge's bench is set apart from spectators by a curved wooden railing, and is set with candles in tall holders. A thirty-star American flag hangs on the wall behind the bench. Twelve captain's chairs await a jury. Attorneys' and clerks' tables hold quill pens, early documents, candles in long holders, and law books that belonged to Judge Davis. A cast-iron stove stands near the juror's box; there are pew-like benches for the spectators. At the rear is a small jury room and judge's office.

When you visit, take a moment to slide into a spectator's bench and absorb the atmosphere. It takes but little imagination to hear Lincoln's high-pitched voice saying, "It's like some of the glib talkers you and I know, Judge . . ."

Several events are held at Mt. Pulaski Courthouse during the year, including ceremonies commemorating Lincoln's birthday on or near February 12. In December, the courthouse is decorated for the holidays.

Mt. Pulaski (pop. 1,600)

With its historic town square, wide streets, and Victorian buildings, Mt. Pulaski is typical of the small rural towns that dot the Illinois prairie. Founded in 1836, it was named for Revolutionary War hero Count Kasimir Pulaski. The "First Lady of Radio," Vaughn DeLeath, an early twenties and thirties radio singer closely associated with the song "Red Sails in the Sunset" was born here. The community celebrates Count Pulaski's birthday in early March and hosts a fall festival with a parade, carnival, and entertainment the second week in September.

HISTORIC MUSEUM AND RESEARCH CENTER:

Located in a former saloon and adjacent bank building across the street from the courthouse, the museum exhibits local history artifacts, including items the saloon gave away to customers, vintage clothing, school memorabilia, and historical documents, highlighted by a land grant signed by President Andrew Jackson in 1829. The research center holdings include genealogical material, local and country histories, an extensive newspaper file, and various histories of Logan County. Located at 104 E. Cooke Street, the museum is open Tuesday through Saturday noon-4, closed Sunday and Monday. Admission: free, donations welcome. Additional information: tel. 217-792-3719.

Nearby Accommodations:
See Lincoln, Illinois, or Springfield, Illinois.

Additional Information:
Abraham Lincoln Tourism Bureau of Logan County,
303 Kickapoo, Lincoln, IL 62656; tel. 217-732-8687.
www.logancountytourism.org/

Metamora Courthouse State Historic Site

Metamora, Illinois

Left: Metamora Courthouse State Historic Site, Metamora, IL.
Right: Museum exhibit, Metamora Courthouse State Historic Site, Metamora, IL.

Location: 113 E. Partridge Street, adjacent to town square; Woodford County.

Hours: Open Tuesday-Saturday 9-12:00 and 1-5; closed New Year's Day, Martin Luther King, Jr. Birthday, Presidents' Day, General Election Day, Veterans Day, Thanksgiving, and Christmas.

Admission: Suggested donation.

Accessibility: Lower level wheelchair accessible.

Information: Metamora Courthouse State Historic Site, 113 E. Partridge, Metamora, IL 61548; tel. 309-367-4470. www.state.il.us/hpa/

Getting There: Metamora is 14 miles northeast of Peoria on Route 116.

The oldest surviving courthouse from the days of the Eighth Judicial Circuit, Metamora was the third stop for Lincoln and his colleagues on their semiannual tour of the circuit. Facing a shady village green surrounded by brick streets, the old courthouse, with its white-columned portico and round-roofed cupola, is a classic example of the Greek Revival style of architecture that was so popular in Illinois in the mid-nineteenth century. Metamora Courthouse was placed on the National Register of Historic Places in 1978.

Metamora Courthouse State Historic Site, Metamora, IL.

What Happened Here

Metamora became the Woodford County seat in 1843 when county headquarters were moved here from the village of Versailles. A local contractor, David Irving, designed and built the courthouse in 1845 at a cost of $4,400. Irving baked his own bricks in a kiln west of the village, felled trees in the nearby forest, and had them cut into timbers for joists and planks for flooring at a nearby sawmill.

Several of the attorneys Lincoln faced in the Metamora courtroom also went on to great fame, among them Adlai E. Stevenson (Vice President of the United States under Grover Cleveland

1893-1897) and Robert Green Ingersoll, known in later life as "the great agnostic"; his lectures on religion won wide attention. Judge David Davis, a long-time associate and friend, became Lincoln's campaign manager during the 1860 presidential campaign. As President, Lincoln named Davis to the U.S. Supreme Court in 1862.

Of the many cases Lincoln tried at Metamora, one has become part of the Lincoln legend. It is confirmed in the Common Law Record Book of 1857-61.

On October 10, 1857, Lincoln was set to defend a seventy-year-old woman named Melissa Goings, charged with murdering her seventy-seven-year-old husband who, Mrs. Goings claimed, was choking her when she grabbed a piece of stove wood and fractured his skull.

Restored courtroom, Metamora Courthouse State Historic Site, Metamora, IL.

When the case was called to trial in the afternoon, Melissa Goings could not be found. What happened remains unclear, but according to the court's bailiff, one Robert Cassell, Lincoln took advantage of a private conference to suggest that she flee.

Confronted by the bailiff when Goings could not be found, Lincoln is reported to have said, "I did not run her off. She wanted to know where she could get a drink of water, and I told her there was mighty good water in Tennessee." Melissa Goings was never again seen in Illinois, and no serious attempt was made to apprehend her. On May 24, 1859, the murder charge was ordered stricken from the court docket.

Woodford County was no longer part of the Eighth Judicial Circuit after 1857, but Metamora survived as county seat and its court continued with full dockets until 1894, when county headquarters were moved to Eureka. Thereafter, the building was used for church suppers, school graduation exercises, civic meetings, social functions, and similar gatherings, and was extensively remodeled. The judge and jury chambers became kitchens, and two wings were added, one for village office space, the other to house Metamora's fire truck. The building became state property in 1921.

The building's exterior and the second floor courtroom have been restored to their 1846 appearance. The lower level, divided by a long corridor leading to the courtroom stairs at the rear, formerly held county offices and is now a museum. Exhibits on the Eighth Judicial Circuit include reproductions of court documents and legal notices from area newspapers. A display on the Metamora House, where Lincoln, other lawyers, and the judge often stayed when court was in session, includes photos of the old hotel and a cupboard, hall tree, chair, dining table, china, cutlery, and other items used there. Other exhibits display early firearms, period clothing, tools, and documentation of Woodford County's participation in the Civil War. Two items are worthy of special note. One is a handmade banner resembling an American flag that was made for the Lincoln-Douglas debates in 1858. The other is a long leather-topped walnut table that was used for meetings during the 1860 presidential campaign. Lincoln, whose customary place was at the side of the table, could not get his long legs underneath, so a section of the side panel was cut away to give him room.

Cutaway Lincoln table, Metamora Courthouse State Historic Site, Metamora, IL.

The second-floor courtroom is a dandy. Worn floorboards creak at each step. Pew-like spectator's benches sit above the floor on risers. A picket-fence railing separates court officials from spectators. The high judge's bench is reached by three steps from either side. A dozen captain's chairs line the jury box and the attorneys' tables, furnished with quill pens and documents, face each other across the room. A thirty-star American flag hangs on one wall. At the rear of the room, on either side, are the tiny jury room and judge's chambers.

Only a judge, jury, and an attorney in a stovepipe hat seem to be missing. One wonders if old Mrs. Goings ever made it to Tennessee.

Attorney's table, Metamora Courthouse State Historic Site, Metamora, IL.

Metamora (pop. 2,500)

Metamora was called Hanover when the county seat was moved here in 1843. But it was discovered there was another Hanover in Illinois (Jo Daviess County), and the village was renamed Metamora, said to be an Indian word meaning "King Philip."

Nearby Accommodations:

Family Fountain Cafe, 112 N. Davenport Street, tel. 309-367-4983.

Myers Homestead Restaurant, 110 E. Mount Vernon Street, tel. 309-367-2328.

Additional Information:

Metamora Village Clerk, 100 N. Davenport Street, Metamora, IL 61548; tel. 309-367-4780.

NO MOON AT ALL
★*May 7-8, 1858*

BEARDSTOWN COURTHOUSE

Beardstown, Illinois

Beardstown Courthouse, Beardstown, IL, site of the famous "Almanac Trial."

LOCATION: 101 W. Third Street; Cass County.

HOURS: Open Monday-Friday 9-5; closed Saturday, Sunday, holidays, and when court is in session.

ADMISSION: Free.

ACCESSIBILITY: Not wheelchair accessible.

INFORMATION: Beardstown Chamber of Commerce, 121 N. State Street, Beardstown, IL 62618; tel. 217-323-3271.

GETTING THERE: Beardstown is 45 miles west of Springfield on Route 125.

Set on the corner of the public square, Beardstown's red brick courthouse—now the City Hall—was built in 1844, when Beardstown was the Cass County seat. It was the scene of the famous Lincoln Almanac Trial. The courtroom has been restored to its 1844 appearance and, while Beardstown is no longer the county seat, court is still held here on Tuesday and Friday. It is the only courtroom in which Lincoln practiced law that is still used for its original purpose. The city council also uses the room for its regular meetings.

Site of Lincoln's Beardstown speech, August 12, 1858.

What Happened Here

Lincoln made many visits to Beardstown. In 1832 he helped pilot the steamer Talisman down the Sangamon River from New Salem to Beardstown. Soon after, his Black Hawk War company was enrolled in state service here. Although it was not part of the Eighth Judicial Circuit, Lincoln argued many cases in the Cass County Circuit Court, including the famous Almanac Trial.

William ("Duff") Armstrong was the son of Hannah and Jack Armstrong, old friends of Lincoln from his New Salem days. Jack could claim a certain notoriety as the leader of the Clary's Grove boys and the man Lincoln wrestled shortly after his arrival in New Salem (see New Salem, Illinois). But Jack and Hannah became Lincoln's close friends during the New Salem Days.

In August, 1857, Duff Armstrong got into a drunken brawl with James H. Norris and James P. Metzker at a camp meeting revival in Mason County, Illinois. Norris struck Metzker with a heavy piece of wood and Armstrong was said to have struck him with a slugshot, a type of metal blackjack. Injured, Metzker mounted his horse and rode away, although he fell from the horse several times. He died three days later. Norris and Armstrong were arrested and indicted for murder in October, 1857.

Norris, who had previously killed another man, was quickly tried in the Mason County seat of Havana, Illinois, convicted of manslaughter, and sentenced to eight years in prison at Alton, Illinois.

Hannah, by then a widow, appealed to her old friend Lincoln to help her son and he set aside a busy schedule (he was campaigning against Stephen A. Douglas for the Illinois senatorial seat) do so. Armstrong's trial began in Beardstown on May 7, 1858.

Charles Allen, the prosecution's star witness, testified he had seen Armstrong strike the fatal blow at ten or eleven o'clock in the evening. While about 150 feet away, Allen said he could see clearly by the light of the moon overhead.

But Lincoln then produced an almanac that showed the moon was low on the horizon at the time Allen said it was high overhead, and would not have provided enough light for him to clearly see what happened. After a doctor testified Metzker could have died from injuries caused by falling off his horse, and another witness stated the slugshot belonged to him and was in his possession the night of the fight, the jury declared Armstrong not guilty.

It was an emotion-filled trial, and there is some speculation in some corners that Lincoln defended a man he knew was guilty of murder, using not only the almanac, but his power of persuasion with the jury to win Armstrong's freedom.

Lincoln did not charge Hannah Armstrong for his services. It is said that after the trial Lincoln gave Duff a short lecture on taking care of his mother and making a man of himself.

Armstrong enlisted in the army during the Civil War. In 1863 President Lincoln—again answering an appeal from Hannah Armstrong, who had one son killed in the war and another wounded—obtained Duff's discharge from the military. Duff Armstrong died in Cass County, Illinois, in 1899, and is buried in the New Hope/Walkers Grove Cemetery near Easton, in adjoining Mason County. His grave marker and a small sign referring to the Almanac Trial are badly weathered and barely discernable.

Lincoln returned to Beardstown during his U.S. Senate campaign with Stephen A. Douglas and on August 12, 1858, spoke to a crowd in the public square. The platform he spoke from faced Second Street. Douglas spoke the previous day, from a platform facing Third Street, and the Republicans, not wanting Lincoln to use the same platform, built another at the north end of the square facing the river.

When the Cass County seat was transferred to the village of Virginia, in 1872, the Beardstown courthouse was used as a school and community hall, and later became the city hall. But court continued to be held here, and the courtroom has been in continuous use since 1844. The jail where Duff Armstrong languished while awaiting trial still exists, but is not open to the public.

The courtroom, on the second floor of the City Hall, was restored to its 1844 appearance in the 1940s. (Modern facilities such as electricity, plumbing, and telephones were maintained.) The court furnishings are reproductions. However, the railing that separates court officials from spectators is original. One can almost picture Lincoln pacing before it, thumbing through the almanac he used to win the Armstrong case.

A copy of an almanac for the year 1857 is on display. During the Armstrong trial, Lincoln, who wore a white Holland suit, had his photo taken by a local photographer. A copy of the photo—the only formal photo taken of Lincoln in a white suit—is on exhibit in the courtroom.

A small museum to the rear of the courtroom has exhibits of antique firearms, Native American spear points and arrowheads, dishes owned by the family of Thomas Beard, who founded the city in 1819, photos, early fashions, and other local history items. Admission: Free.

Beardstown, Illinois (pop. 5,200)

Built on the site of Kickapoo Town, once a famous Indian mound village, Beardstown is located at Mile 88 above the mouth of the Illinois River and is today a bustling river town. River Walk is an ongoing riverfront development project in progress, and the foot of Main Street is a fine place to watch the comings and goings of barge and towboat traffic on the Illinois River.

Historical Markers

Lincoln Speech Site: A boulder with a bronze plaque on the north side of the public square marks the site of Lincoln's 1858 campaign in Beardstown.

Schmoldt Memorial Park: One of Lincoln's earliest visits to Beardstown was at the outbreak of the Black Hawk War, when the rag-tag Sangamon County company encamped near the Illinois River in the vicinity of what is now Schmoldt Memorial Park. It was here that Lincoln was elected company captain. A historical marker indicates the spot. From the public square, follow Second Street east to Wall Street, then turn north to reach the park.

Beardstown's annual Fall Fun Festival, held the fourth weekend of September each year, draws thousands of people to enjoy good food, crafts, a parade, games, carnival rides, and entertainment from nationally known country music performers.

Nearby Accommodations:
Mascouten Motel, R.R. 1, Springfield Road, Beardstown, IL 62618; tel. 217-323-2552.

Super 8 Motel (42 rooms), Hwy 67 and 100, Beardstown, IL 62618; tel. 217-323-5858.

Star Cafe, intersection of Route 67 and 125, tel. 217-323-9869.

Riverview Restaurant, 218 W. Main, tel. 217-323-9808.

Additional Information:
Beardstown Chamber of Commerce, 121 North State Street, Beardstown, Illinois 62618; tel. 217-323-3271.
www.beardstown.org/

★August-October 1858

The Lincoln-Douglas Debates

The 1858 race for Illinois' U.S. Senate seat launched Abraham Lincoln to national fame. Even today it is better known than many national presidential campaigns. Senator Stephen A. Douglas, the incumbent, had held the seat for a decade and was perhaps the best known American politician of his time. But he was hated in many quarters for his Kansas-Nebraska Act and, coupled with his blatantly racist attitudes toward slavery, it was felt that he might be vulnerable to a strong Republican candidate.

Lincoln, despite having received 110 votes for Vice President at the Republic National Convention in 1856, was not especially well known outside of Illinois. Nor was his following especially strong in parts of his own state, particularly the southern region known as "Little Egypt," where proslavery sentiments ran high.

When the Republican State Convention nominated Lincoln as its "first and only candidate for United States Senator," on June 16, 1858, it marked the first time in Illinois history that a senatorial candidate had been nominated. But the nomination was not binding and Lincoln's name appeared on no ballot. Senators were chosen by their state legislatures, not by popular vote, so the real battle in the contest was for the eighty-seven seats in the Illinois legislature.

Lincoln began the campaign with his "House Divided" speech in Springfield, delivered the evening of his nomination. In Washington, Douglas, on learning of Lincoln's nomination, said, "I shall have my hands full . . . He is as honest as he is shrewd, and if I beat him my victory will be hardly won."

Douglas began his campaign in Chicago on July 9, delivering a speech from the balcony of the Tremont House. Lincoln addressed a large crowd from the same balcony the following evening.

It was Republican strategy that Lincoln speak soon after Douglas and draw on the Little Giant's crowds whenever possible. Furthermore, Northern Illinois was considered a Republican stronghold. Southern Illinois—wedged between the slave states of Missouri and Kentucky—was solid Douglas territory. The crucial area was central Illinois, where settlers had both Southern and Northern backgrounds. Lincoln would concentrate his campaign efforts there.

Both candidates spoke at separate gatherings in Springfield on July 17. But the Republicans felt Lincoln must confront the Little Giant face to face. On July 24, Lincoln sent Douglas the following letter from the Tremont House in Chicago:

CHICAGO, ILL., JULY 24, 1858

HON. S. A. DOUGLAS.
MY DEAR SIR: WILL IT BE AGREEABLE TO YOU TO MAKE AN ARRANGEMENT FOR YOU AND MYSELF TO DIVIDE TIME, AND ADDRESS THE SAME AUDIENCES THE PRESENT CANVASS? MR. JUDD, WHO WILL HAND YOU THIS, IS AUTHORIZED TO RECEIVE YOUR ANSWER; AND, IF AGREEABLE TO YOU, TO ENTER INTO THE TERMS OF SUCH AGREEMENT.

YOUR OBEDIENT SERVANT,
A. LINCOLN

Douglas, who had little to gain, could not refuse a challenge. In accepting, he suggested the series be limited to seven debates, one in each of the seven Congressional Districts where they had not appeared together. Beginning in August, they would meet in Ottawa, Freeport, Jonesboro, Charleston, Galesburg, Quincy, and Alton. Lincoln agreed; the stage for the great debates was set.

But the campaign was not limited to the formal meetings. Both candidates went on the stump before, during, and after the debates. At Clinton, where Douglas spoke for three hours on the afternoon of July 27, Lincoln appeared in the evening and delivered his famous maxim, "You can fool all of the people part of the time and part of the people all of the time, but you cannot fool all of the people all of the time." A life-size statue of Lincoln by the Belgian artist Van den Bergen marks the spot at the DeWitt County Courthouse in Clinton.

The campaign was grueling by any standards. Braving the heat of late summer and early autumn, Lincoln spoke at Henry, Augusta, Macomb, Urbana, Sullivan, Bloomington, Danville, Decatur, Galesburg, Havana, Lewiston, Monmouth, Tremont, Mt. Sterling, Beardstown, Carthage, and scores of other locales. Douglas made appearances in fifty-seven Illinois counties and gave 113 speeches, many as long as three hours.

In Sullivan, where the candidates also spoke the same day, a near-riot ensued when Lincoln and Douglas supporters clashed in the public square. Here, and at dozens of other places where Lincoln and/or Douglas spoke, plaques, markers, and boulders commemorate the spot.

THE SCHEDULE IS SET
★*July 29, 1858*

BRYANT COTTAGE STATE HISTORIC SITE

Bement, Illinois

Bryant Cottage State Historic Site, Bement, IL.

LOCATION: Corner of Wilson Street and Route 105; Piatt County.

HOURS: Open daily 9-5 March-October, 9-4 November-February; closed New Year's, Martin Luther King, Jr. Birthday, Presidents' Day, Veterans Day, Thanksgiving, and Christmas Day.

ADMISSION: Donation suggested.

ACCESSIBILITY: Wheelchair accessible.

INFORMATION: Bryant Cottage State Historic Site, P.O. Box 41, 146 E. Wilson Street, Bement, IL 61813; tel. 217-678-8184.

GETTING THERE: Bement is located 30 miles southwest of Champaign. From I-72, take Exit 63 to Route 105, then proceed seven miles south to Bement.

Tradition holds that Lincoln and Douglas met in this tiny, four-room, white frame cottage to work out the final details for their debates. The diminutive house was built in 1856 for Francis E. Bryant, a Bement merchant and banker and a close friend of Stephen A. Douglas. Senator and Mrs. Douglas were houseguests here on July 29 and 30, when Douglas spoke at nearby Monticello.

What Happened Here

Following his speech at Monticello, Douglas returned to Bement, where he was to catch a train the following day. Shortly after leaving Monticello, Douglas and his entourage met Lincoln, who was on his way to the town. The candidates stopped and held a short roadside conference. Lincoln is said to have told Douglas he had a reply to the Little Giant's letter of July 24th, agreeing to debates and locations, although he had not yet compared the original with his copy. Douglas told him to send the letter to Bement; the two shook hands and departed. Lincoln made his speech at Monticello, then returned to Bement and caught the midnight train to Springfield.

A plaque along Route 105, two miles south of Monticello, marks the spot where Lincoln and Douglas held their roadside chat. Another, on the courthouse lawn in Monticello, commemorates Lincoln's travels to Piatt County on the old Eighth Judicial Circuit.

While there is no documented proof, Bryant family tradition has long held that Lincoln and Douglas met in the parlor at Bryant Cottage the evening of July 29. And a letter Douglas sent Lincoln from Bement on July 30, setting specific dates for the debates and saying, "I agree with your suggestion that we shall alternatively open and close the discussion," suggests that they discussed the upcoming meetings in greater detail than their brief roadside encounter would have allowed.

The Bryant family kept the cottage parlor open to the public until 1947, when the house was donated to the State of Illinois.

The cottage has a tiny kitchen, a combination sitting room-dining room, a bedroom, and the small parlor where Lincoln and Douglas met. The rooms have lovely period furnishings and antiques, including a yarn weasel (used to wind yarn into skeins) and a child's rocking chair original to the home. The parlor contains a horsehair couch and chair and other Eastlake-style Victorian furnishings.

Special events at the cottage include a Lincoln tribute (on or about February 12), Bement Day, a July 4th Freedom Celebration, and a Holiday Open House.

Another exciting day in Bement took place in August of 1955 when actress Marilyn Monroe visited the community during its centennial celebration.

Nearby Accommodations:
See Decatur, Illinois.

★August-October 1858

The Great Debates

Because of Douglas's fame, the debates generated wide coverage. Newspapers large and small in cities throughout the country carried extensive accounts of the joint meetings. Southern papers in places like Louisville and Frankfort, Kentucky, Charleston and Columbia, South Carolina, Norfolk, Mobile, New Orleans, Wilmington, North Carolina, and Columbus, Georgia, offered coverage, comment or, more often, criticism.

Politics in nineteenth-century Illinois had an air of the spectacular, which the debates raised to even greater heights. Railroads throughout the Midwest offered reduced fares and special trains to the debates, attracting both Democratic and Republican delegations, which came, literally, by the carload. In St. Louis and Hannibal, Missouri, and Keokuk, Iowa, packet boats ran special excursions to Quincy and Alton.

At Ottawa, the dust stirred up by the crowd coated both candidates. Douglas was met at Freeport with thundering cannon, rifle salutes, bands, and a huge torchlight parade. Lincoln rode, somewhat unwillingly, from the Brewster House to the debate site in a Conestoga wagon pulled by six horses. Douglas walked. At Charleston, Lincoln's carriage was followed by a wagon filled with thirty-two young ladies, each representing a state in the Union. Douglas backers in Quincy formed a parade some two miles long. Everywhere there were bands, banners, glee clubs, marching cadets, and thousands of onlookers.

Douglas traveled in style, in a private railroad car decorated with banners and signs, accompanied by his beautiful wife, his secretaries, stenographers, and a retinue of followers. Coupled to his train was a flatcar with a brass cannon, which two young men fired as the train approached each town. Lincoln often traveled on the same train, riding as an ordinary passenger.

Douglas dressed as he traveled, usually wearing a wide-brimmed white hat, a ruffled shirt, and a dark coat with shining buttons, light trousers, and shined shoes (the Republicans called it his "plantation outfit." He was the orator—shouting, threatening, accusing, shaking his fist as he spoke. Lincoln, in black, with rough boots and the familiar top hat, had a high-pitched voice that grew shrill when he was excited. He was awkward on the platform and to emphasize a point, often bent his knees and body with a sudden downward jerk, then shot up to his full height.

There were no public address systems and the candidates had to make themselves heard by ten thousand or more people. By the end of the campaign, Douglas's voice was nearly gone. Lincoln seemed unaffected by the grind. In seven three-hour debates, Lincoln and Douglas reached but a tiny fraction of the people who saw or heard John Kennedy and Richard Nixon in only one of their televised debates in 1960. But by all accounts, the 1858 Lincoln-Douglas debates for the Illinois senate seat made the Kennedy-Nixon debates in the 1960 presidential campaign, and those that have since followed, look like small potatoes.

Ottawa, Illinois
LaSalle County
August 21, 1858

Some twelve thousand people stirred up great clouds of dust as they milled about the public square where the first debate was held.

Douglas began, accusing Lincoln of conspiring to destroy the Whigs, dissolve the Democrats, and start a new party disguised as Republicans whose goal was to emancipate blacks and make them the political and social equals of whites. He hammered hard at fears of black equality, and raised seven questions that he demanded that Lincoln answer. Lincoln, on the defensive, said the physical difference between the black and white races would "probably" always keep them from living in perfect equality. Further, he said, while blacks were not his equal or Douglas's equal in moral and intellectual endowment, they were equal to "every living man" in their right to life, liberty, and the pursuit of happiness, including the right to the fruits of their labor.

When it was over, cheering Republicans carried Lincoln off on their shoulders. The following day, Lincoln told a newspaper editor, with obvious relief, "Douglas and I, for the first time this canvass, crossed swords here yesterday; the fire flew some and I am glad to know I am yet alive."

Ottawa, Illinois (pop. 17,500)

The site of this debate is marked by a permanently-lighted boulder and plaque in Washington Park, at the corner of Jackson Street and Route 23, in the center of town. Elsewhere in the park is a memorial to W. D. Boyce, the Ottawa native who founded the Boy Scouts of America. Adjacent to Washington Park, at 100 Lafayette Avenue, is the Reddick Mansion, which stood here at the time of the debates. It houses the offices of community organizations, including the Chamber of Commerce. Some restored rooms in the mansion are open to tours.

A historical marker near the intersection of Route 71 and 23 indicates the location of Fort Johnston where, on May 27, 1832, Lincoln enlisted as a private in Elijah Iles' company—his second enlistment in the Black Hawk War.

Additional Information:

Ottawa Visitors Center, 100 W. Lafayette Street, Ottawa, IL 61350; tel. 888-OTTAWA-4 or 818-434-2737.
www.visit-ottawa-il.com/

Freeport, Illinois
Stephenson County
August 27, 1858

Fifteen thousand people jammed into Freeport on a damp and chilly day for the second and most famous of the debates.

Lincoln began by answering the questions Douglas raised at Ottawa, saying he was not in favor of unconditional repeal of the Fugitive Slave Law; not against the admission of more slave states into the Union; not against the admission of a new state with such a constitution as the people of that state saw fit to make; not pledged to abolish slavery in the District of Columbia; not pledged to prohibit slave trade between the states; was pledged to the right and duty of Congress to prohibit slavery in all United States territories; and not against the honest acquisition of new territories, even if slavery were not first prohibited there.

Lincoln then went on the offensive, asking Douglas: Could the people of a territory "in any lawful way" exclude slavery before statehood? And, if the Supreme Court ruled that a state could not prohibit slavery, would Douglas abide by the decision?

Douglas's reply became known as the Freeport Doctrine. Yes, he said, the people of a territory could exclude slavery before statehood simply by refusing to enact the necessary protective measures. As to the Supreme Court, Douglas was certain it would never hand down any such decision as Lincoln described, saying it would be "an act of moral treason."

Douglas's answers did not sit well in Southern states. Some historians believe they cost him the presidential election in 1860.

Freeport, Illinois (pop. 25,800)

A boulder and plaque dedicated in 1903 by President Theodore Roosevelt marks the debate site at the corner of Douglas Street and State Avenue. A statue of a seated Lincoln and a standing Douglas, called "Lincoln and Douglas in Debate," the work of sculptress Lilly Tolpo of Stockton, Illinois, was dedicated at the site on August 27, 1992, the 134th anniversary of the debate.

The statue, "Lincoln the Debater," by the sculptor Leonard Crunelle, was presented to Freeport at the seventy-first anniversary of the Freeport debate on August 27, 1929, by local industrialist W. T. Rawleigh. Refurbished and rededicated in 2000, it is located in Taylor Park, 900 E. Stephenson Street. From the debate site, follow Route 75 east three-quarters of a mile to the park entrance.

The Stephenson County Historical Society, housed in an 1857 stone house at 1440 S. Carroll Avenue, has local history exhibits and nineteenth-century furnishings. Museum hours are Wednesday-Sunday noon-4, May-October, Friday-Sunday noon-4 rest of the year. Admission: Adults, $3.00; age 6 and up, $1. Additional information: tel. 815-232-8419.

Right: Lincoln-Douglas debate site, Freeport. President Theodore Roosevelt dedicated the boulder in 1903.

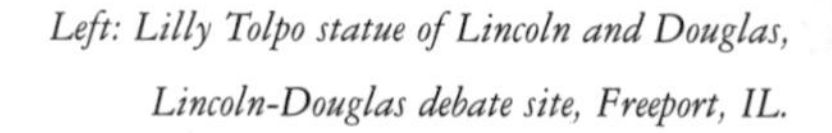

Left: Lilly Tolpo statue of Lincoln and Douglas, Lincoln-Douglas debate site, Freeport, IL.

Additional Information:

Stephenson County Convention & Visitors Bureau, 2047 AYP Road, Freeport, IL 61032; tel. 1-800-369-2955 or 815-233-1357. www.stephenson-county-il.org/ex3.html

JONESBORO, ILLINOIS
UNION COUNTY
SEPTEMBER 15, 1858

The third debate, at Jonesboro, was in the section of southern Illinois known as Little Egypt, located farther south than Richmond, Virginia. Many of the fifteen hundred people who attended were Buchanan Democrats, opposed to both candidates.

Douglas performed well for his Southern audience, saying that the Republican Party was boldly abolitionist in northern Illinois, "bleached and . . . paler" in central Illinois, and "in this neighborhood" content to talk "about the inexpediency of the repeal of the Missouri Compromise." In his highly racist speech Douglas said, "I hold that this government was made on the white basis, by white men, for the benefit of white men and their posterity forever, and should be administered by white men and none others."

Lincoln, knowing the Republicans could never carry the district, quoted numerous Democratic resolutions from Illinois, which urged excluding slavery from the territories. He argued that popular sovereignty, Douglas's idea for settling slavery in the territories, would not work because the Supreme Court in the Dred Scott decision made it unlawful to exclude slave property from a territory. He did not comment on Douglas's white supremacy remarks.

Douglas received enormous cheers from the partisan crowd. In the autumn elections, the Republicans did not even run any candidates for the state legislature in the district.

Jonesboro, Illinois (pop. 1,780)

A boulder and plaque marks the site of the third Lincoln-Douglas debate in Jonesboro City Park.

Additional Information:

Southernmost Illinois Tourism Bureau, P.O. Box 278, Ullin, IL 62992; tel. 800-248-4373.
www.southernmostillinois.com/southernindex.htm

Charleston, Illinois
Coles County
September 18, 1858

More than twelve thousand people gathered for the fourth debate at the Coles County Fairgrounds. Lincoln, apparently bothered by Douglas's statements on racial equality at Jonesboro, began by saying he was not and never had been in favor of social and political equality of the white and black races, that he did not favor making voters or jurors of blacks, qualifying them to hold office, or intermarrying with whites.

Douglas, in reply, accused Lincoln of racial hypocrisy, saying of the Republicans, "Their principles in the north are jet-black, in the center they are in color of a decent mulatto, and in lower Egypt they are almost white . . . Thus, they avow one set of principles up there, they avow another and entirely different set down here . . . Lincoln maintains that the Declaration of Independence asserts that the Negro is equal to the white man, and that under Divine Law, and if he believes so, it was rational for him to advocate Negro citizenship, which, when allowed, puts the Negro on an equality under the law. I say to you in all frankness, gentlemen, that in my opiniona Negro is not a citizen, cannot be, and ought not to be, under the Constitution of the United States."

Lincoln desperately wanted to put the racial issue aside, but Douglas simply would not let it be.

GALESBURG, ILLINOIS
KNOX COUNTY
OCTOBER 7, 1858

Despite a raw, windy day, more than fifteen thousand people gathered on the Knox College campus in Galesburg to hear the candidates speak from a platform erected at Old Main. It may have been the largest audience at any of the debates.

Douglas hammered away against racial equality at the onset, saying, ". . . I tell you this Chicago doctrine of Lincoln's—declaring that the Negro and the white man are made equal by the Declaration of Independence and Divine Providence—is a monstrous heresy. The signers of the Declaration of Independence never dreamed of the Negro when they were writing that document."

In reply, Lincoln raised the issue of Douglas's declaration that he "don't care whether slavery is voted up or down," by saying, ". . . you will see at once that this is perfectly logical, if you do not admit that slavery is wrong. If you do admit it is wrong,

Judge Douglas cannot logically say he don't care whether a wrong is voted up or down." Regarding Douglas's assertion that the Declaration of Independence did not apply to blacks, Lincoln said, "Judge Douglas and whoever, like him, teaches that the Negro has no share, humble though it may be, in the Declaration of Independence, is going back to the era of our liberty and independence, and, so far as in him lies, muzzling the cannon that thunders its annual joyous return . . . he is blowing out the moral lights around us when he contends that whoever wants slaves has a right to hold them."

Left: Steven A. Douglas plaque, Old Main, Knox College, Galesburg, IL.

Right: Old Main, Knox College, site of the Galesburg Lincoln-Douglas debate. The famed "Lincoln Window" is to the left of the door.

Galesburg, Illinois (pop. 33,500)

Old Main, on the Knox College campus at the corner of South and Cherry Streets, is the only debate site that remains much as it was in 1858, and was designated a National Historic Landmark in 1936. Lincoln and Douglas spoke from a platform on the east side of the building, where plaques commemorate the event. The debate was moved to the east side of Old Main at the last minute, to shelter the speakers from a brisk west wind. Because it was not made for the building, the speakers' platform blocked the door and Lincoln, Douglas, and other officials were forced top climb out through a window.

Lincoln is said to have remarked that he had "finally gone through college." The "Lincoln Window," as it known, is to the immediate left of the door and is now part of the office of the President of Knox College.

The three-room cottage where Pulitzer Prize-winning poet and Lincoln biographer Carl Sandburg was born is open to visitors. On the grounds is Remembrance Rock, his gravesite. The cottage, at 331 E. 3rd Street, is open 9-5 daily; closed New Year's, Day, Martin Luther King, Jr. Birthday, Presidents' Day, Veterans Day, General Election Day, Thanksgiving, and Christmas. Admission: Suggested donation.
Additional information: tel. 309-342-2361.

Carl Sandburg Cottage State Historic Site, Galesburg, IL.

Additional Information:
Galesburg Area Convention and Visitors Bureau, 2163 E. Main Street, Galesburg, IL 61401; tel.; 309-343-2485.
www.visitgalesburg.com/

QUINCY, ILLINOIS
ADAMS COUNTY
OCTOBER 13, 1858

The sixth debate took place literally within site of the slave state of Missouri, across the Mississippi River from Quincy. Some ten thousand people crowded around the public square on a chilly, windy day.

Lincoln continued to accent the moral issues of slavery, summarizing positions he had taken at Freeport, Jonesboro, and Galesburg, and saying that Douglas had "the high distinction, so far as I know, of never having said slavery is either right or wrong." The Republicans, he said, "think it is a moral, a social, and a political wrong . . . we also oppose it as an evil so far as it seeks to spread itself."

Douglas responded by saying, "He tells you that I will not argue the question of whether slavery is right or wrong. I tell you why I will not do it. I hold that, under the Constitution of the United States, each State of the Union has a right to do as it pleases on the subject of slavery . . . If we stand by that principle, then Mr. Lincoln will find that this Republic can exist forever, divided into Free and Slave States, as our fathers made it, and the people of each State have decided."

Quincy, Illinois (pop. 42,500)

A monument marking the debate site stands in Washington Park, at the corner of Maine and Sixth Streets in downtown Quincy. The work of famed Illinois sculptor Lorado Taft, the huge bronze relief is mounted on a block of granite and depicts the debate platform, portraying Lincoln as tall and strong, Douglas, short and stout.

Additional Information:
Quincy Convention and Visitors Bureau, 300 Civic Center Plaza, Suite 237, Quincy, IL 62301-4161; tel. 800-978-4748 or 217-223-1000. www.quincy-cvb.org/

Alton, Illinois
Madison County
October 15, 1858

The seventh and last debate, at Alton, was more or less anticlimactic, possibly because extensive press coverage of the previous meetings had satisfied people's curiosity about what the candidates had to say. Only about five thousand people gathered in front of the City Hall to hear Lincoln and Douglas conclude their debates.

Douglas, now so hoarse that it hurt him to speak, again accused Lincoln and the Republicans of holding different political creeds in different parts of the state and insisted his position was consistent throughout the debates.

". . . whenever the time arrives that I cannot proclaim my political creed in the same terms, not only in the Northern, but the Southern part of Illinois, not only in the Northern, but the Southern States, and wherever the American flag waves over American soil, then there must be something wrong with that creed . . . I now again assert, that in my opinion our Government can endure forever, divided into Free and Slave States as our fathers made it—each State having the right to prohibit, abolish, or sustain slavery, just as it pleases."

Lincoln-Douglas Debate Site, Alton, IL.

Responding, Lincoln said, "The real issue in this controversy—the one pressing upon every mind—is the sentiment on the part of one class that looks upon the institution of slavery as a wrong, and of another class that does not look upon it as wrong." Then it was over.

Alton, Illinois (pop. 33,000)

The debate site, now called Lincoln-Douglas Square, stands are the corner of Market and Spring Streets, overlooking the Mississippi River, and features full size bronze replicas of Lincoln and Douglas.

A neatly stacked pile of limestone rock at the corner of Broadway and Williams Streets, in downtown Alton, marks the site of Illinois' first penitentiary, later an infamous Civil War prison camp where, it is estimated, between one thousand and five thousand Confederate prisoners of war died.

Additional Information:

Greater Alton/Twin Rivers Convention and Visitors Bureau, 200 Piasa Street, Alton, IL 62202; tel. 800-258-6645 or 618-465-6676. www.altoncvb.org/

Election Day, November 7, dawned cold and rainy. Republican legislative candidates in Illinois polled four thousand more votes than their opponents, but an outdated apportionment law, which favored the Democratic southern districts of the state, and holdover Democrats in the legislature reassured Douglas's election. In the final tally, the Illinois Legislature was made up of fifty-four Democrats and forty-six Republicans. Despite the months of hard campaigning, Lincoln lost again.

Keenly disappointed, Lincoln was still able to write an old friend, "I am glad I made the late race. It gave me a hearing on the great and durable question of the age, which I could have had in no other way; and although I now sink out of view, and shall be forgotten, I believe I have made some marks which will tell for the cause of civil liberty long after I am gone."

GOOSENEST PRAIRIE FARM
★1840-1892

LINCOLN LOG CABIN STATE HISTORIC SITE

Lerna, Illinois

Lincoln Log Cabin State Historic Site, Lerna, IL.

LOCATION: Twelve miles south of Charleston on Lerna Road; Coles County.

HOURS: Historic site open daily 8:30-dusk year-round; the Visitors Center open 9-5 daily, April-October, 9-4 daily rest of the year. The Living History program operates 9-5 daily, May-October. Closed New Year's Day, Presidents' Day, Veterans Day, Thanksgiving, and Christmas.

ADMISSION: Suggested donation.

ACCESSIBILITY: Rough paths lead to the farm site.

INFORMATION: Lincoln Log Cabin State Historic Site, R.R. 1, P.O. Box 175, Lerna, IL 62440; tel. 217-345-6489.

GETTING THERE: Exit I-57 at Route 16 toward Charleston; at first stoplight turn south on Lerna Road and follow site markers twelve miles south to the cabin.

This site marks the Goosenest Prairie Farm that was the last home of Abraham Lincoln's father and stepmother, Thomas and Sarah Bush Lincoln. This is a living history farm where first-person interpreters perform household and farm chores of the 1840s and play the roles of the people who lived here.

Lincoln Log Cabin State Historic Site, Lerna, IL.

What Happened Here

Thomas Lincoln, discouraged after the brutal Macon County winter of 1830-31, set out for Indiana in the spring of 1831. En route, he stopped in Coles County, Illinois, some sixty-five miles southeast of Decatur, where he decided to settle and give Illinois another chance. The family lived on three farms in the county before Thomas purchased the Goosenest Prairie Farm in 1840.

Being Southerners, the Lincolns preferred log houses to frame houses. The Goosenest Prairie house was a double-room, "saddle-bag" style cabin that was common in Kentucky. It was essentially two log cabins, built close to each other end-to-end, with the space between boarded over.

In 1845 there were eighteen people living in the Lincoln home. These included, besides Thomas and Sarah, Sarah's son, John D. Johnston, and his wife, Mary; their six children; Sarah's daughter, Matilda, and her husband, Squire Hall; and their six children. The quarters must have been crowded, to say the least.

Sometime after 1845, Squire Hall purchased a farm about a mile south of the Lincolns and moved his family there. John Johnston, on the other hand, was a lazy sort who was always coming up with "get-rich-quick" schemes that never worked.

Although he had labored most of his life, Thomas Lincoln, at age sixty-two, was little better off in 1840 than he was thirty years earlier at Sinking Spring Farm in Kentucky, where Abraham was born. He now had four times as many mouths to feed and farming was still a matter of back-breaking drudgery with age-old tools. Thomas raised corn, oats, and wheat. His livestock included hogs, sheep, milk cows, horses, chickens, and geese. Pork, potatoes, and cornbread were the staples in the family diet and these were supplemented with wild game, orchard produce, and garden vegetables in season.

By 1841, Thomas owned 120 acres in Illinois, but he still faced hardscrabble times. Within a year he had to sell a third of his land to Abraham to get out of financial difficulty. In 1848, Thomas asked Abraham for twenty dollars to keep the rest of his land from forced sale.

Although Abraham Lincoln visited Coles County often, especially between 1841 and 1848, when he did a good bit of business in nearby Charleston, his visits to Goosenest Prairie were infrequent. During an interview in 1865, seventy-seven-year-old Sally Lincoln recalled that after her stepson left home on his own, she "saw him every year or two." Lincoln did not come to his dying father's bedside nor did he attend his funeral. When Thomas Lincoln died in 1851, he had never met his daughter-in-law or seen his grandchildren. He is buried in Shiloh Cemetery, a mile from the cabin.

Lincoln returned to Coles County for the last time on January 30, 1861. He missed rail connections at Mattoon, so the President-elect of the United States rode part of the way in the caboose of a freight train, spending the night with old lawyer friends in Charleston.

The next day he drove a buggy twelve miles south to the home of his stepsister, Matilda, who was by then Mrs. Ruben Moore. There he spent the day with Sally Lincoln, holding his stepmother's hand as they talked about times past and times to come. He visited the Johnstons and the Hankses (Dennis's family), who had been so much a part of his Kentucky and Indiana years, and sometime that day said a silent farewell to Thomas Lincoln in Shiloh Cemetery.

Original Thomas Lincoln grave marker, Shiloh Cemetery, Lerna, IL.

One cannot help but wonder about the family's feelings that day. Lincoln, barely a month from the Presidency, with six states seceded from the Union and more certain to follow, riding a freight train to bid farewell to the family that had seen him through times almost too painful to remember. Sally, who first saw Lincoln in Indiana, the day she moved into the cabin at Little Pigeon Creek, when Abraham and his sister had to be dressed up to look "more human." And Hanks, who had held the crying Lincoln the February morning he was born in Kentucky, who helped build Nancy Hanks Lincoln's coffin, who lived with Abraham in squalor at Pigeon Creek and survived with him the winter of the "big snows" in Macon County. Now Abraham was leaving to become President of the United States. Surely their emotions ran high.

Sally rode with Lincoln back to Charleston, where there was a reception with friends and acquaintances that evening. Stepmother and stepson said an emotional goodbye the next day, and Lincoln boarded a train for Springfield.

Four years and two months later, they came to tell Sally that Abraham was dead. In an 1865 interview with William Herndon, Lincoln's law partner and biographer, Sally said, "I did not want

Abe to run for President and I did not want to see him elected . . . When he came down to see me, after he was elected President . . . my heart told me . . . that I should never see him again."

Sally Lincoln died at the Goosenest Prairie farm on April 10, 1869, at the age of eighty-one. She is buried beside Thomas in Shiloh Cemetery.

With Thomas's death in 1851, ownership of the farm passed to John D. Hall, Sally's grandson, who lived in the cabin until it was moved to Chicago and displayed at the Columbian Exposition in 1893. Afterwards, it was put in storage and eventually disappeared.

An accurate replica of the Lincoln cabin was constructed its original sites after the State of Illinois acquired the farm in 1929. Both rooms are furnished with items and artifacts from the 1840s and '50s, although none of the items are known to have belonged to the Lincolns. In 1976, an 1840s farm was reconstructed around the cabin. A garden, orchard, and farm crops are planted with varieties typically found on the Illinois prairie in the mid-nineteenth century. Split-rail fences surround farm fields and livestock such as Thomas Lincoln kept roam the fields. There is an original nineteenth-century log barn, moved here from southern Illinois in 1981. A smoke house, corn crib, well, and root cellar are modern reconstructions based on what was commonly found on an 1840s farm. The well and root cellar are original from the ground down.

Interpreters dressed in period clothing perform the day-to-day chores farm chores of the period, planting and harvesting farm crops, chopping wood, sewing, spinning, and cooking meals in the cabin fireplace using 1840s recipes. The interpreters play first-person roles, assuming that of an original member of the Lincoln family or a nearby neighbor. Speaking in the Southern Upland dialect common in eastern Illinois in the 1840s, they tell you about their lives and the times here, but always from the viewpoint of the character they portray.

In contrast to the Lincoln cabin is the Sargent Farm, a quarter-mile away, which was opened to visitors in 1989. Originally located ten miles from the Lincoln farm, it was the home of Stephen Sargent, an industrious New Englander. While Thomas Lincoln practiced subsistence farming, Sargent was a progressive farmer who kept up with the newest innovations in agriculture. The Sargent farm features an 1844 timber frame house and log outbuildings, including stables, a corn crib, a smokehouse, and a summer kitchen. The house is furnished with artifacts from the period.

The site has a large, modern Visitors Center with exhibit galleries highlighting the Lincolns and Sargents as well as the artwork of some of Illinois' more prominent artists. A gift shop offers books, crafts, and other items relating to the Lincoln Log Cabin.

A number of special events are held at the Visitor Center or on the two farms during the year.

Nearby Accommodations:
See Charleston, Illinois.

Ruben Moore Home State Historic Site: Located one mile west of the Lincoln Log Cabin on Lerna Road, in the remnants of the settlement of Farmington, is the nineteenth-century frame house that was the home of Mrs. Ruben Moore, who was Sally Lincoln's daughter, Matilda. It was here that Lincoln came to visit his stepmother for the last time in early 1861. The small home has period furnishings and artifacts. Outdoor signage tells the history of the community of Farmington.

Ruben Moore Home State Historic Site, Lerna, IL, where President-elect Lincoln paid a farewell visit to his stepmother.

Shiloh Cemetery: Located on Lerna Road near the Moore Home, this peaceful country cemetery adjacent to the old red brick Shiloh Church is the final resting place of Thomas and Sarah Bush Lincoln. A weather-worn, lichen-stained stone, topped by a small obelisk and surrounded by an iron fence, is inscribed:

THOMAS LINCOLN
FATHER OF
MARTYRED PRES.
BORN
JAN. 6, 1778
DIED
JAN. 15, 1851

LINCOLN

Thomas and Sarah Bush Lincoln grave site, Shiloh Cemetery, Lerna, IL.

Nearby, in a plot surrounded by an iron fence, Thomas and Sally lie side by side, their graves marked with modern stones and a granite memorial erected by area service organizations.

Nearby Accommodations:
See Charleston, IL.

Charleston, Illinois (pop. 20,400)

In March, 1864, six soldiers and three civilians were killed in Charleston in a riot that occurred when a local Democratic Congressman was to give a speech. It was the largest battle fought between soldiers and civilians in the North over an issue other than the draft. Fifteen of the rioters were imprisoned in Fort Delaware, Delaware. In November, 1864, President Lincoln ordered the fifteen returned to Coles County. Thirteen were released, and two stood trial in Illinois, only to be released. A marker on the lawn of the Coles County Courthouse, at Monroe Avenue and 7th Street, commemorates the "Charleston Riot."

Dennis Hanks, Lincoln's cousin, who lived with the Lincoln family from 1817 to 1831, settled in Charleston when Thomas and Sally Lincoln moved to Coles County. While Lincoln was President, Hanks and John D. Hall, Sally's grandson, argued over the responsibility of caring for Lincoln's aging stepmother. Lincoln sent Hanks fifty dollars for her care. In May, 1864, Hanks visited Lincoln in Washington to discuss Sally Lincoln's welfare and to plead for the release of those arrested in the Charleston riot.

Hanks was a cobbler by trade. After Lincoln's death, he joined John Hanks (another Lincoln cousin) in purchasing and exhibiting the Macon County cabin in which Lincoln had lived briefly. William Herndon, in preparing his biography of Lincoln, interviewed Hanks in person and carried on a long correspondence with him. While Hanks' tales did not always ring true, much of what is known about Lincoln's Kentucky and Indiana years can be attributed to him. Hanks was killed in 1892, run down by a carriage in Charleston. He is buried in the Old Chambers Cemetery, which is near the intersection of Madison Avenue and B Street on the west side of the city.

Lincoln-Douglas Debate Museum: Opened in the summer of 2000, the museum is a work in progress and a needed addition to the chronicles of the debates. Museum exhibits focus on the seven debates, with emphasis on the Charleston Debate, and include a mural reproduction and a scaled diorama of the biggest day in Charleston's history. Seven panel displays take you through the events preceding and leading to the Charleston

Debate. A Coles County exhibit depicts the role that Lincoln played in Charleston and Coles County (see Lincoln Log Cabin State Historic Site). A video shown in the museum's small auditorium uses footage from C-Span's 1994 re-enactments of the debates to vividly dramatize what took place here. The museum is located just inside the east gate of the Coles County Fairgrounds, corner of 'E' Street and Madison Avenue, where the Charleston Debate was held. Open daily 10-4. Admission: free, donation suggested. Additional information: Charleston Tourism, 501 Jackson Avenue, Charleston, IL; tel. 217-348-0430.

Lincoln-Douglas Debate Museum, Charleston, IL.

Nearby Accommodations:

Best Western Worthington Inn (67 rooms), 920 W. Lincoln Avenue, Charleston, IL 61920; tel. 217-348-8161.

Days Inn, 710. W. Lincoln Avenue, Charleston, IL 61920; tel. 217-345-7689 or 800-DAYS-INN.

Friends & Co., 509 Van Buren, tel. 217-345-2380.

K. L. Krackers, 1405 4th Street, tel. 217-348-8343.

Additional Information:

Charleston Area Chamber of Commerce, Visitor Information Center, 501 Jackson, Avenue, Charleston, IL 61920; tel. 217/348-0430 or 217/345-7041. www.charlestontourism.org/

Related Lincoln Sites in Illinois

Bloomington, Illinois (pop. 57,000)

The state Republican Party was formally organized in Bloomington in 1856 at a convention called to protest the Kansas-Nebraska Bill, which made possible the westward expansion of slavery. It was at that convention that Abraham Lincoln delivered his "Lost Speech," so called because no record of it was kept. Several of Lincoln's close associates were residents of Bloomington, including Jesse Fell, Leonard Swett, and David Davis, all of whom had much to do with helping Lincoln gain the Republican nomination for President. Fell, in 1859, requested an autobiography from Lincoln to be used in the East, where people knew little about him. It is one of the more important sources of information on Lincoln's family and early life.

David Davis Mansion State Historic Site: Davis was born in Maryland in 1815 and settled in Bloomington in 1836. He met Abraham Lincoln shortly after, and the two became legal and political associates, as well as close friends. Davis was elected judge of Illinois' Eighth Judicial Circuit in 1848 and Lincoln practiced before him for the rest of his years on the circuit, at times presiding over the court when the judge was absent (see Eighth Judicial Circuit). Davis organized the forces that nominated Lincoln at the Republican National Convention in Chicago in 1860 and campaigned vigorously for Lincoln's election. President Lincoln appointed Davis to the U.S. Supreme Court in 1862.

"Cloverlawn," David Davis Mansion State Historic Site, Bloomington, IL.

The Davis mansion, "Clover Lawn," was constructed in 1872 of yellow brick with stone quoins in the corners. The lavish Victorian home has eight marble fireplaces and boasted many modern features for its time, including central heating and indoor plumbing. Many furnishings are original.

Clover Lawn is open Thursday-Monday 9-5 (last tour begins at 4 P.M.); closed New Year's, Martin Luther King, Jr. Birthday, Presidents' Day, General Election Day, Veterans Day, Thanksgiving, and Christmas Day. Admission: Suggested donation. Additional information: David Davis Mansion State Historic Site, 1000 East Monroe St. Bloomington, IL 61701; tel. 309-828-1084. www.state.il.us/hpa/

MCLEAN COUNTY MUSEUM OF HISTORY:
Located in the former McClean County Courthouse, the museum offers three floors of galleries and exhibits, along with demonstrations, lectures, and programs. In the Politics Gallery you'll discover McClean County's long history of political involvement and meet such famous politicians as Abraham Lincoln, David Davis, and Adali Stevenson. On the east lawn of the museum is the Lincoln Statue Bench, a life-size, cast-bronze statue of Lincoln seated on a bench, by artist Rick Harney. With room enough for visitors to sit with Lincoln, the statue is rapidly becoming one of central Illinois' most popular. Located at 202 N. Main Street, the museum is open Monday-Saturday 10-5 (until 9 P.M. Tuesdays), Sunday 1-5; closed New Year's Day, Memorial Day, Fourth of July, Labor Day, Thanksgiving, and Christmas Day. Admission: $2 adult; $1 age 12 and under, free admission on Tuesdays. Additional information: tel. 309-827-0428; www.mchistory.org

Bloomington, with its twin city of Normal, is home to Illinois Wesleyan University, which has galleries, theaters, and athletic events open to the public. Two Adlai Stevensons made Bloomington their home—Adlai I, a contemporary of Lincoln's who traveled with him on the Eighth Judicial Circuit, and who was Vice President of the United States under Grover Cleveland—and Adlai II, his grandson, who was Governor of Illinois, U.S. Ambassador to the United Nations, and twice the Democratic candidate for the Presidency. The Stevenson graves are in Evergreen Cemetery, on Miller Street, just east of the 1100 block of S. Main Street.

Additional Information:
Bloomington-Normal Area Convention and Visitors Bureau, 210 S. East Street, P.O. Box 1586, Bloomington, IL 61701-1586; tel. 800-433-8226 or 309-829-1641. www.visitbn.org/

Chicago, Illinois (pop. 2,784,000)

The Wigwam, a huge, temporary wooden structure in which Abraham Lincoln was nominated for the Presidency at the National Republican Convention in 1860, stood at what is now the corner of Lake Street and Wacker Drive. A historical marker on the southeast corner of the intersection marks the site. In Lincoln Park, along Lakeshore Drive from North Avenue to Hollywood Avenue, is a majestic statue of Lincoln by the famed sculptor, Augustus Saint-Gaudens. It depicts Lincoln standing in deep contemplation, having risen from a chair to speak. Grant Park, on the lakefront between Randolph street and McFetridge Drive, has a Saint-Gaudens statue of a seated Lincoln.

Douglas Tomb State Historic Site: Lincoln's long-time political adversary, Stephen A. Douglas was perhaps the best known politician of his era. He and Lincoln first met in the old statehouse in Vandalia, in 1834, and battled each other across Illinois for the next twenty-five years, arguing both state and national issues. Their famous debates during the U.S. Senate race in 1858 brought Lincoln national political fame, although Douglas won the election (see Lincoln-Douglas debates).

Five feet four, Douglas was known as the Little Giant, both for his deep voice and his aggressive, rough and tumble style of politics. He was elected to the Illinois legislature in 1836, but resigned to become Register of the Springfield Land Office. He was Illinois Secretary of State from 1840 to 1841, and Judge of the Illinois Supreme Court from 1841 to 1843. In 1843, he was elected to Congress, serving three terms in office. Douglas won election to the U.S. Senate in 1847, and was reelected in 1858. He ran for President in 1860, but lost the election to Lincoln.

Douglas, in Washington when Confederate forces fired on Fort Sumter, hurried to the White House to offer President Lincoln his support. Douglas announced he was solidly behind the President and the Union, then hurried home to rally Illinois Democrats to the Union cause. He died in Chicago on June 3, 1861, at the age of forty-eight.

Douglas's tomb was designed by Chicago sculptor Leonard W. Volk, whose wife was Douglas's cousin. The ninety-six-foot-high granite and marble structure is adorned with statues and symbolic art depicting Douglas's contributions to the state and the nation. Flag-lowering ceremonies are held on Sunday evenings during the summer months. The tomb, at 636 E. 35th Street, is open daily 9-5; closed New Year's, Thanksgiving, and Christmas. Admission: Free. Additional information: tel. 312-225-2620. www.state.il.us/hpa/

LEARNING MORE ABOUT LINCOLN

CHICAGO HISTORICAL SOCIETY: A House Divided: America in the age of Lincoln is a major Lincoln exhibit that uses paintings, photos, documents and artifacts from the society's priceless collection to examine the political and social forces of mid-nineteenth-century America—the institution of slavery, the extraordinary territorial expansion of the country, the fierce sectionalism of free and slave economies, and the massive destruction and suffering caused by the Civil War.

A sampling of artifacts displayed are the bed on which Lincoln died; the table on which Lincoln signed the Emancipation Proclamation; Abraham Lincoln's letter to Stephen A. Douglas setting the terms for the 1858 debates; Lincoln's Civil War letter to General Grant saying, "Let the thing be pressed; and an original copy of the Thirteenth Amendment abolishing slavery, signed by Lincoln.

The society's collections include the silk and beaver top hat which Lincoln wore to his 1861 inauguration ceremony, a carriage that Lincoln owned, Lincoln's watch and spectacles, and a bronze bust, life mask, and hands of Lincoln by the Chicago sculptor Leonard Volk, and a vast number of other Lincoln artifacts.

The society is located at the south end of Lincoln Park at Clark Street and North Avenue. All galleries and public areas are wheelchair accessible. Exhibition galleries and the museum store are open Monday through Saturday 9:30-4:30, Sunday noon-5, closed major holidays. Admission: Adults $5; ages 65 and up, and students age 13-22, $3; ages 6-12, $1. Additional information: Chicago Historical Society, Clark Street at North Avenue, Chicago, IL 60614-6099; tel. 313-642-4600. www.chicagohistory.org/

Additional Information About Chicago:
Chicago Office of Tourism, Cultural Center, 4th Floor, 78 E. Washington, Street, Chicago, IL 60602; tel. 312-744-2390. www.cityofchicago.org/tourism/

Danville, Illinois (pop. 37,700)

Danville was the home of Ward Hill Lamon (1828-1893), an attorney who in the 1850s traveled the Eighth Judicial Circuit with Lincoln and Judge David Davis. Lamon was Lincoln's Vermilion County associate from 1852 to 1857, and worked for Lincoln's election to the U.S. Senate in the 1845 and 1858 campaigns. He was one of many Republicans who toiled for Lincoln's presidential nomination and election, and he accompanied the President-elect on his inaugural journey to Washington.

Lincoln appointed Lamon Marshall of the District of Columbia in 1861. As such, Lamon served as local prisonkeeper, performed ceremonial duties, and occasionally acted as the President's bodyguard. He was Marshall-in-chief of the procession at Gettysburg before Lincoln's 1863 address and introduced Lincoln from the platform. Lamon resigned as Marshall of the District of Columbia in 1865 and entered practice with a Washington law firm.

In 1869 he acquired copies of William Herndon's research notes on Lincoln for two thousand dollars and a two thousand dollar note. His partner's son then wrote a biography of Lincoln, using Herndon's research materials, Lamon's name, and Lamon's memories of Lincoln. Lamon's *Life of Abraham Lincoln* often painted Lincoln in a negative light; it was not well received and sold less than two thousand copies.

Vermilion County Museum: The museum is housed in an 1855 Victorian home that is listed on the National Register of Historic Places. Abraham Lincoln spoke from the home's balcony on September 21, 1858, during his campaign for the Illinois Senate seat. The Lincoln room, where Lincoln slept after attending a Danville political meeting, contains the original canopied bed in which Lincoln slept and the fireplace, floor, and woodwork that were in the room during his visit, and other Lincoln memorabilia. The museum also has several rooms filled with local history exhibits.

Located at 116 N. Gilbert, the museum is open Tuesday-Saturday 10-5, Sunday 1-5; closed Monday and holidays. Admission: Adults $2; ages 6-14, 50¢.

The historical society also owns and operates the Lamon House, built in 1850 by Joseph Lamon, a cousin of Ward Hill Lamon's. It is believed that Lincoln occasionally stayed at the white frame cottage when he stopped at Danville while riding the Eighth Judicial Circuit. The home, located in Lincoln Park, is open Sunday 1:30-4, May through October; closed the rest of the year. Additional information: Vermilion County Historical Society, tel. 800-383-4386 or 217-442-2922.

A Danville landmark is the Danville Soldier's Monument, created by Illinois sculptor Lorado Taft, which stands at the corner of Main and Gilbert Streets.

Additional Information:
Danville Area Convention and Visitors Bureau
101 W. Main, #146, Danville, IL 61834;
tel. 800-383-4386. www.danvillecvb.com/index.ace

Dixon, Illinois (pop. 15,100)

Abraham Lincoln was here several times during his service in the Black Hawk War. The Lincoln Monument State Memorial marks the site of the Fort Dixon blockhouse erected during the war. Here, it is said, the future Presidents Abraham Lincoln and

Zachary Taylor, and the future Confederate President, Jefferson Davis, all met in 1832. Other men of prominence who served here were: General Winfield Scott, 1852 Whig Presidential nominee and famous soldier; Robert Anderson, the Union officer in charge of Fort Sumter, South Carolina, when the Civil War broke out; Albert Sidney Johnson and Joseph E. Johnson, Civil War generals for the Confederacy; William S. Hamilton, son of Alexander Hamilton; and John Reynolds, Illinois governor.

Leonard Crunelle statue, "Lincoln the Soldier," Lincoln Monument State Memorial, Dixon, IL.

Overlooking the Rock River, this small park features the statue "Lincoln, the Soldier," by the sculptor Leonard Crunelle. It is the only statue depicting Lincoln in military uniform. A historical marker details Lincoln's Black Hawk War career. The memorial is located on Lincoln Statue Drive, between Galena and N. Hennepin Avenues, on the north bank of the river at the Route 26 bridge.

RONALD REAGAN BOYHOOD HOME: President Ronald Reagan, born in nearby Tampico, grew up in Dixon. His boyhood home at 816 S. Hennepin Avenue has been restored and furnished to appear as it did when he lived here from 1920 to 1923. Guided tours are offered Monday-Saturday 10-4, Sunday 1-4, April–November, Saturday and Sunday only, December-March. Admission: free. Additional information: Tel. 815/288-3404.

Additional Information:
Dixon Chamber of Commerce, 101 W. Second Street, Dixon, IL 61021; tel. 815-284-3361. www.dixonil.com/visitors.htm

Galena, Illinois (pop. 3,600)

Galena, once the center of the Illinois lead mining region, has been visited by many prominent figures that had close associations with Lincoln. In 1832 Jefferson Davis, then a lieutenant in the U.S. Army, stopped here while transporting the vanquished warrior, Black Hawk, to Jefferson Barracks, Missouri, at the conclusion of the Black Hawk War.

Abraham Lincoln first visited this old Northwestern Illinois mining town in June, 1832, while a soldier in the Black Hawk War. His most famous visit was on July, 23, 1856, when he spoke while campaigning for John C. Fremont for President, addressing a gathering from the balcony of the DeSoto House, then the "largest and most luxurious hotel in the West." Galena was a campaign stop for Stephen A. Douglas during the U.S. Senate race in 1858. Ulysses S. Grant used the DeSoto House as his headquarters during the 1868 presidential campaign. A state historical marker on the front of the extensively-remodeled hotel, at the corner of Main and Green Streets, commemorates the events.

A West Point graduate, Grant was employed in his father's leather store in Galena when Fort Sumter fell in 1861. He marched off to war, returning in triumph four years later as the commander-in-chief of the Union Armies. In all, nine Galena men who served in the Union Army during the Civil War reached the rank of general.

U.S. Grant Home State Historic Site: The home was presented to Grant by the grateful citizens of Galena on August 18, 1865, when he returned to Galena as the victorious Civil War General. Grant lived here until elected President, in 1868, and again briefly in 1879. Constructed in 1859, the Italianate brick home contains many of Grant's possessions, including china and silver used in the White House. Tours are offered daily, with evening candlelight tours offered on special weekends in the summer and autumn. Located at 500 Bouthillier Street, the Grant Home is open daily 9-5 (last tour begins at 4:45); closed New Year's Day, Martin Luther King, Jr. Birthday, Presidents' Day, Veterans Day, General Election Day, Thanksgiving Day, and Christmas Day. Admission: Suggested donation. Additional information: tel. 815-777-3310. www.state.il.us/hpa/

U.S. Grant Home State Historic Site, Galena, IL.

Galena/Jo Daviess County Historical Museum: Housed in a beautiful Italianate brick home built in 1858, the museum features a large area of Civil War exhibits that include original weaponry, letters, prints, and photos. A highlight is Thomas Nast's famous oil painting "Peace in Union" (9 x 12 feet) depicting Lee's surrender to Grant at Appomattox. Other local history exhibits recall Galena's lead mining and steamboating heritage. Located at 221 Bench Street, open daily 9-4:30; closed Easter, Thanksgiving, Christmas Eve, Christmas Day, New Year's Eve, and New Year's Day. Admission: Adults $4; ages 10-18, $3; under age 10 free with an adult. Additional information: tel. 815-777-9129. www.galenahistorymuseum.org

Galena is noted for some of the finest period architecture in the Midwest; most of the community's downtown section is listed on the National Register of Historic Places. A statue of Grant stands in Grant Park.

Additional Information:
Galena/Jo Daviess County Convention and Visitors Bureau, 101 Bouthillier Street, Galena, IL 61036; tel. 818/777-4390 or 800-747-9377. www.galena.org/

Kent, Illinois

The Black Hawk War Monument, located some two miles east of this hamlet, was erected and dedicated in 1886 to honor those killed in the Black Hawk War. The monument stands on the former site of Kellogg's Grove, a tiny settlement established in 1827 on a mail route between Peoria and Galena.

Black Hawk War Monument, Kellogg's Grove, near Kent, IL.

Here, on June 25, 1832, a small force of soldiers commanded by Major John Dement clashed with a party of Sauk Indians commanded by Black Hawk. Five soldiers and six Indians were killed in the skirmish. The next day Captain Jacob M. Early's spy company, of which Lincoln was a member, arrived on the scene. According to George M. Harrison, a Springfield friend of Lincoln's who also served in the company, "The only part we could then act, was to seek the lost men, and with hatchets and hands to bury them." According to tradition, Lincoln helped bury the slain soldiers, apparently where they fell.

Fifty years after the Black Hawk War, area farmers began a movement to collect the remains of soldiers buried throughout the area and enshrine them in one location with a fitting monument. They were reburied at the base of a 34-foot high monument, which was erected at the grove on a hill overlooking Yellow Creek Valley. The site includes picnic areas, a shelter, playground, and a log cabin that was moved here in 1981. Listed on the National Register of Historic Places, Kellogg's Grove marks the final battle of the Black Hawk War in Illinois. The site is open from dawn to dusk.

Kellogg's Grove is some fifteen miles west of Freeport. From the intersection of U.S. 20 and Illinois Highway 73, just south of Lena, go west on U.S. 20 for three miles and turn south on Kent Road (there's a sign). The monument is three miles south of U.S. 20.

Additional Information:
Stephenson County Convention & Visitors Bureau, 2047 AYP Road, Freeport, IL 61032; tel. 800-369-2955 or 815-233-1357. www.stephenson-county-il.org/index3.html

Lawrenceville, Illinois (pop. 4,900)

The Lincoln Trail State Memorial is located nine miles east of Lawrenceville on U.S. 50, near the western end of the Lincoln Memorial Bridge, opposite Vincennes, Indiana. The imposing memorial is set in a thirty-one acre park that marks the place where the Lincoln family entered Illinois on March 6, 1830.

Erected in 1938, the monument is the work of Nellie Verne Walker, of Red Oak, Iowa, and consists of a twenty-six by nine-foot sculpted limestone panel set on a six-foot-high granite base. Figures carved in four-inch relief on the face of the panel depict the Lincoln family entering Illinois in an ox-drawn covered wagon. A lifelike statue of a young Lincoln, goad in hand, appears to be walking along beside the oxen.

Lincoln campaigned in southern Illinois on behalf of William Henry Harrison for President in 1840. While in Lawrenceville he had a dispute with a local physician, William G. Anderson, who the previous August had run as a Democrat and lost the election for State Representative. In writing to Lincoln, Anderson said that Lincoln was the "aggressor" in the dispute and that his "words imported insult." A plaque on the courthouse lawn in Lawrenceville commemorates the event.

Polo, Illinois (pop. 2,514)

On August 15 through 17, 1856, Lincoln was a guest at the home of Zenas Aplington, the founder of this northern Illinois community. On Saturday, August 16, Lincoln and Aplington were joined by John D. Campbell and James W. Carpenter, who were law partners in Polo, in a carriage drive to Oregon, the Ogle County seat. There Lincoln and "Long John" Wentworth, six-term Illinois Congressman and later Mayor of Chicago, were among the speakers at a political rally for John C. Fremont, the first Republican Presidential candidate.

Aplington House, Polo, IL. Lincoln was a guest here in August, 1856.

The two-story frame house holds exhibits on Polo's history, including Lincoln's 1856 visit. Located at 123 N. Franklin Street, the home is open by request during normal business hours.

Stop at the Blackhawk Waterways Convention & Visitors Bureau office, which is across the street.

Additional Information:
Blackhawk Waterways Convention & Visitors Bureau, 201 N. Franklin Avenue, Polo, IL 61064; tel. 800-678-2108 or 815-946-2274. www.blackhawkwaterwayscvb.org/

Stillman Valley, Illinois (pop. 961)

This Ogle County village was the site of the Battle of Stillman's Run, on May 14, 1832, the first engagement of the Black Hawk War and a defeat for the volunteer forces. Lincoln helped bury several militia men killed here and long remembered the event (see New Salem, Illinois). A soaring marble monument commemorating the battle is inscribed with the words: "The presence of the soldier, statesman, martyr Abraham Lincoln, assisting in the burial of these honored dead has made this spot more sacred." The graves of the eleven soldiers who died in the battle are beside the monument.

Battle of Stillman's Run Monument, Stillman Valley, IL.

U.S. Grant Home State Historic Site, Galena, IL. The silver service is from the Grant White House.

Additional Information:
Blackhawk Waterways Convention & Visitors Bureau, 201 N. Franklin Avenue, Polo, IL 61064; tel. 800-678-2108 or 815-946-2274. www.blackhawkwaterwayscvb.org/

EPILOGUE

ABRAHAM LINCOLN *(1809-1865)*

Abraham Lincoln's assassination was a black milestone in American history. On April 14, 1865, he was shot by Southern sympathizer John Wilkes Booth while watching a performance of Our American Cousin, at Ford's Theatre in Washington, D.C. He died at 7:22 the following morning, at the William Petersen House, across the street from the theater where his unconscious form had been carried. Lincoln's assassination, the first of an American President, caused an outpouring of national shock and rage that was unsurpassed until the assassination of President John F. Kennedy, in 1963. The entire country was draped in black. Men met on the street, silently touched each other's hands, and broke into tears.

There were heavy hearts in the South, as well, for it was understood that the new President, Andrew Johnson, would deal much more harshly with the rebels than would have Abraham Lincoln. Jefferson Davis, fleeing from Union troops as the Confederacy collapsed, later wrote of his feelings when informed of Lincoln's death. "The news was to me very sad, for I felt that Mr. Johnson was a malignant man, and without the power or generosity which I believed Mr. Lincoln possessed." General Robert E. Lee at first refused to hear the details of Lincoln's murder. He had surrendered the Army of Northern Virginia as much to Lincoln's goodness as to Grant's artillery, he said, and regretted Mr. Lincoln's death as much as any man in the North.

On Wednesday, April 19, the official funeral services were held in the East Room of the White House. Six hundred attended—sixty clergymen in all, Cabinet members, the Supreme Court justices, important officials, foreign Ministers, the new President, Andrew Johnson, and General Grant. Mrs. Lincoln, still indisposed, was not present, but Robert Lincoln came. Grant, the tough, battle-hardened, seemingly emotionless soldier who led the Union to victory for Lincoln, wept.

Lincoln's remains were then taken to lie in state in the Capitol Rotunda. Sixty thousand spectators jammed the mile-long route; forty thousand walked in the funeral procession.

The Capitol doors were opened at ten o'clock on the morning

of April 20. Special consideration was given to soldiers from the convalescent hospitals—pale, weak, and wounded men, many of whom limped past the coffin on crutches, some in uniforms with empty sleeves. Afterwards came the general public, in a mile-long line, at times three thousand to the hour. At midnight, when the great Capitol doors were closed, more than twenty-five thousand had said goodbye to the President.

On Friday morning, April 21, Lincoln's coffin was placed on a black-draped funeral train for a circuitous, 1,662-mile journey to Springfield. There were stops in Baltimore, Harrisburg, Philadelphia, New York City, Albany, Buffalo, Cleveland, Columbus, Indianapolis, and Chicago. At each stopover, the coffin was removed from the train and taken to a place of honor for public viewing and funeral ceremonies.

All along the route where the cortege did not stop, flags flew at half-mast, buildings were draped in black, bells tolled, guns were fired, and floral arches spanned the tracks. At night, bonfires and torches were lit. The train, which traveled at twenty miles per hour for the entire route, slowed to five miles per hour at every station it passed. The engineman tolled his bell continuously through these stations and towns.

The funeral train finally pulled into Springfield at 9 A.M. on Wednesday, May 3. Thousands of silent onlookers crowded the prairie capital's streets as the coffin, in an elaborate hearse drawn by six black horses, was taken to the Hall of Representatives in the State Capitol. At ten o'clock, the Capitol doors were thrown open. An estimated seventy-five thousand people passed the open coffin on its magnificent catafalque during the twenty-four hour visitation.

On Thursday, May 4, 1865, funeral services were held in Oak Ridge Cemetery. The "most grand and solemn funeral pageant the world had known" came to an end. Abraham Lincoln had come home to Illinois.

Mary Todd Lincoln (1818-1882)

Prone to severe headaches and fits of ill temper, Mary Lincoln performed her duties as First Lady well, although her extravagances were often an embarrassment to her husband. She exceeded an appropriation to redecorate the seedy White House by nearly seven thousand dollars and, fearful of severe scrutiny by Washington society because she had grown up in the West, spent wildly on clothes. She was alternately miserly and extravagant, and hid her enormous debts from the President.

After William Lincoln died in the White House in 1862, Mrs. Lincoln began to change. She never again went into the room where Willie died and was embalmed, and canceled her social activities for a year. She began to consult spiritualists.

President Lincoln's assassination plunged Mary Lincoln into such despair that she took no part in any of the funeral ceremonies, other to insist that her husband be buried at Oak Ridge Cemetery in Springfield. She did not leave the White House for Illinois until May 22, more than a month after Lincoln's death, and moved into a house in Chicago.

In 1866, William Herndon publicly offered his theory that Ann Rutledge, of New Salem, was the one love of Lincoln's life, causing Mary more anguish. Although she despised Herndon, she granted him an interview, held at the St. Nicholas Hotel in Springfield on September 4, 1866. During the long conversation, she spoke lovingly of her husband.

In 1867, obsessed by money problems, she tried to sell some of her old clothes in New York, a humiliating experience that angered her son, Robert. Growing increasingly unstable, Mrs. Lincoln began to shun old friends and often traveled incognito, using false names. She went to Germany with Tad in 1868, returning in 1871. Tad died soon after, and she was again inconsolable.

Mrs. Lincoln began to express unwarranted fears that her son, Robert, would die. She often carried thousands of dollars in negotiable securities on her person. In 1875, after consulting with Lincoln's old friends, Judge David Davis and John T. Stuart, Robert instigated an insanity trial. The court judged his mother insane and committed her to a private sanitarium in Batavia, Illinois.

After less than four months in the sanitarium, Mary was released to the custody of her sister and brother-in-law, Elizabeth and Ninian Edwards, and moved into their Springfield home. A second trial in 1876 judged Mrs. Lincoln sane, and she left that autumn for France. Beset by serious health problems, she returned to the Edwards home in 1880. Mary Todd Lincoln spent the last year of her life alone in a room in the Edwards house, the shades drawn, the room dimly lit by candles. There she died, on July 16, 1882, at the age of sixty-four. She is buried in her husband's tomb at Oak Ridge Cemetery in Springfield.

Robert Todd Lincoln (1843-1926)

Born while his parents lived at the Globe Tavern in Springfield, Robert's relationship with his father was not especially close. Lincoln himself said of Robert that his parents "never controlled him much."

He entered Harvard University in the fall of 1860. He accompanied his father on part of the inaugural trip to Washington, was present for the inauguration, and visited his parents at the White House on vacations. He graduated from Harvard in 1864 and in early 1865 was appointed captain and assistant adjutant general of volunteers on General Ulysses S. Grant's staff. Robert was present at Lee's surrender to Grant at Appomattox. He breakfasted with his father the day Lincoln was assassinated and was at his father's bedside when he died.

Robert was admitted to the Illinois Bar in 1867 and became a successful lawyer, establishing a partnership with Edward Isham in 1872 that became the firm of Isham, Lincoln, and Beale in 1887. The firm kept the name for more than a century, dissolving in 1989.

Robert married Mary Eunice Harlan (1847-1937), the daughter of Iowa Republican politician James Harlan, in 1868. They had three children: Mary (1869-1936), Abraham "Jack" Lincoln II (1873-1890), and Jessie (1875-1948).

Like his father, Robert Lincoln was a staunch Republican and in 1881 was appointed Secretary of War by President James A. Garfield. He was present in the railroad station when Garfield was shot in 1881. In 1889 he was appointed minister to England by President Benjamin Harrison, holding that post until 1893.

In later years Robert became increasingly involved in business, and was president of the Pullman Palace Car Company in Chicago from 1901 to 1911. He paid close attention to what was written and said about his father, controlling Lincoln's Presidential papers. He allowed his father's private secretaries, John Hay and John Nicolay, to use the papers for a Lincoln biography published in 1880, then willed them to the Library of Congress with the stipulation that they not be opened until twenty-one years after his own death. They became available to the public in 1947.

Robert lived to attend the dedication of the Lincoln Memorial in Washington, D.C., in 1922. He died at his summer home at Manchester, Vermont, in 1926, at the age of eighty-three, and is buried in Arlington National Cemetery.

EDWARD BAKER LINCOLN (1846-1850)

The Lincoln's second son was born in the Springfield house at Eighth and Jackson and died there, of a lung ailment, a month before his fourth birthday. He is buried in his father's tomb at Oak Ridge Cemetery.

WILLIAM WALLACE LINCOLN (1850-1862)

Named for his mother's brother, Willie was a studious boy and was thought by Mrs. Lincoln to be a "peculiarly religious child." He fell ill with a fever in 1862 and died at the White House on February 20, at the age of twelve. Willie was buried in Oak Hill Cemetery in the Washington suburb of Georgetown. After Lincoln's assassination, the casket was exhumed and his remains were carried on the Lincoln funeral train to Springfield. He is buried in his father's tomb at Oak Ridge Cemetery.

THOMAS "TAD" LINCOLN (1853-1871)

Perhaps Lincoln's favorite son, Thomas was nicknamed Tad because as a baby he resembled a tadpole with his head too large for his body. He spoke with a lisp and had a serious speech impediment. Undisciplined, he had the run of the White House and kept pets that included a pony and two goats.

After Lincoln's death, Tad was his mother's constant and loving companion. He died of apparent tuberculosis in July 1871, at age eighteen, and is buried in his father's tomb in Springfield.

WILLIAM H. HERNDON (1818-1891)

Lincoln's law partner from 1844 to 1865, Herndon devoted much of his life after Lincoln's death to gathering material for a biography of the slain President. Beginning in 1865, he traveled to eastern Illinois and southern Indiana, researching the early years of Lincoln's life. He interviewed Lincoln's stepmother, his cousin,

Dennis Hanks, and Mary Todd Lincoln. He sent queries by mail, and had lawyer friends interview people who remembered Lincoln. It was Herndon who discovered Lincoln's romance with Mary Owens and the alleged romance with Ann Rutledge.

Deviled by drink and financially pressed, Herndon sold the research notes to his book to Ward Hill Lamon in 1869. In the early 1880s he attempted to get his life in order and, in collaboration with Jesse W. Weik, produced Herndon's *Lincoln: The True Story of a Great Life*, which was published in 1889. The book is still in print.

While the biography contains many inaccuracies, it provides much information about Lincoln's personality and his years in Indiana that cannot be obtained from any other source.

Herndon died two years after his book was published, at the age of seventy-three. He is buried in Oak Ridge Cemetery in Springfield, IL.

Abraham Lincoln's last living descendent was a great grandson, Robert Lincoln Beckwith, the son of Robert's daughter, Jessie Lincoln, and Warren Wallace Beckwith. Twice married, he had no children. His death in December, 1985, at age eighty-one, marked the end of the direct line of Lincoln's descendents.

ADDITIONAL READING

Should you wish to delve more deeply into the life and history of Abraham Lincoln, be forewarned—the subject is highly addictive. Thousands of books have been written on virtually every aspect of Lincoln's life, and there are hundreds more on his associates and friends. The selections listed here are totally subjective, but offer a good, basic profile of the life and times of Abraham Lincoln. Some of the older editions are available as reprints.

Abraham Lincoln: The Prairie Years and the War Years
Carl Sandburg, Harcourt Brace, 1989
Perhaps the best known of Lincoln's biographers, Sandburg's writings are highly lyrical and dramatic, although he perpetuated some of the Lincoln myths.

Abraham Lincoln: The Prairie Years, 2 vols.
Carl Sandburg, Harcourt, Brace, 1926

Abraham Lincoln: The War Years, 4 vols.
Carl Sandburg, Harcourt, Brace, 1939
Sandburg's original six-volume biography of Lincoln occasionally turns up in antiquities bookstores and at the on-line auction services on the Internet.

Lincoln
David Herbert Donald, Simon & Schuster, 1995
A masterful biography, written from Lincoln's point of view.

Abraham Lincoln, A Biography
Benjamin P. Thomas, The Modern Library, 1968
Thomas, a noted Lincoln authority, writes beautifully on a subject he spent a lifetime researching.

Lincoln's New Salem
Benjamin P. Thomas, Southern Illinois University Press, 1987
This short work of 178 pages is considered the definitive work on New Salem. There are maps and line drawings, along with a section on the restoration of the village.

The Last Best Hope of Earth
Mark E. Neely, Jr., Harvard University Press, 1995
A masterful examination of Lincoln's political career.

The Abraham Lincoln Encyclopedia
Mark E. Neely, Jr., Da Capo Press, 1982
The book's encyclopedia format makes it user-friendly; Neely covers a vast array of material in a detailed yet highly readable manner. The book contains many photographs.

Herndon's Life of Lincoln
William H. Herndon and Jesse W. Weik, Da Capo Press, 1983
The 1880s literary style takes some getting used to, and there are some inaccuracies, but the book is listed as a reference in most works on Lincoln. Herndon published material that is unobtainable from any other source.

Honor's Voice
Douglas L. Wilson, Alfred A. Knopf, 1998
Co-Director of the Lincoln Research Center at Knox College, Dr. Wilson makes a fascinating examination of Lincoln's life between 1831 and 1842.

The Lincoln-Douglas Debates
Harold Holzer, ed., HarperCollins Publishers, 1993
Noted Lincoln scholar Holzer presents unedited texts of the debates, warts and all.

Moonlight
John Evangelist Walsh
St. Martin's Press, 2000
Walsh examines the famed Almanac Trial in a different light.

Here I Have Lived
Paul M. Angle, Abraham Lincoln Book Shop, 1971
Angle, a noted Lincoln authority, paints a vivid picture of the Springfield of Lincoln's Day.

Lincoln's Herndon
David Donald, Alfred A. Knopf, 1946
This biography of Lincoln's third law partner and biographer provides fascinating insights into the lives and times of both men.

The Lincoln Reader
Edited by Paul Angle, Rutgers University Press, 1947
Using the works of authors ranging from William Herndon to Carl Sandburg, the book details Lincoln's life from the perspective of many writers.

The Day Lincoln Was Shot
Jim Bishop, Harper & Row, 1955
Bishop, who was famous for his "The Day . . ." series, provides a detailed account of Abraham Lincoln's last day on earth.

We saw Lincoln Shot: One Hundred Eyewitness Accounts
Timothy S. Good, ed., University of Mississippi Press, 1995
Gripping accounts of the assassination by people who were there.

His Name is Still Mudd: The Case Against Dr. Samuel Alexander Mudd
Edward Steers, Jr., Thomas Publications, 1997
Steers explores the Mudd connection with Lincoln's assassination.

Selected Lincoln Publications

Lincoln Herald
Lincoln Memorial University
Cumberland Gap Parkway, Harrogate, TN 37752
http://web.mountain.net/~niddk/

Lincoln Lore
(available with museum membership)
The Lincoln Museum
500 East Berry Street, Fort Wayne, IN 46802
www.thelincolnmuseum.org/index2.html

The Surratt Courier
(available with membership in the Surratt Society)
Surratthouse Museum
9110 Brandywine Road, Clinton, MD 20735
www.surratt.org/su_cour.htm

The Lincoln Chronicle
Illinois Benedictine College
5700 College Road, Lisle, IL 60532

Lincoln Newsletter
Lincoln College, Lincoln, IL 62656

Journal of the Lincoln Assassination
Autograph Press
P.O. Box 380545, San Antonio, TX 78280

Lincoln Organizations

Abraham Lincoln Association
Old State Capitol, Springfield, IL 62701-1507
www.alincolnassoc.com/

Lincoln Association of Indiana
1010 E. 86th Street, Suite 61-J, Indianapolis, IN 46240

Lincoln Fellowship of Wisconsin
413 West Street, Beaver Dam, WI 53916-1557

Lincoln Group of Illinois
Benedictine University
5700 College Road, Lisle, IL 60532-0900

The Lincoln Forum
300 Switch Road, Hope Valley, RI 02832
http://web.mountain.net/~niddk/Forum/

LINCOLN WEB SITES

The Internet has changed all aspects of our lives; historical research is no exception. Only a few Lincoln sites will get you started, since they will link you to other Lincoln sites, which will link you to other sites, which will link you to other Lincoln sites, ad infinitum.

ABRAHAM LINCOLN ONLINE
http://showcase.netins.net/web/creative/lincoln.html
The premier Lincoln site on the web, bar none, with current news from the world of Lincolniana, tours of Lincoln sites, book reviews, author interviews, a lively discussion section, and great links, including many Civil War web sites.

THE ABRAHAM LINCOLN RESEARCH SITE
http://members.aol.com/RVSNorton/Lincoln2.html
Created by a former history teacher, this excellent web site is divided into three parts: The Abraham Lincoln Research Site, the Mary Todd Lincoln Research Site, and Abraham Lincoln's Assassination. Each section contains a vast amount of information, and there's a huge list of Lincoln links.

THE AMERICAN CIVIL WAR HOME PAGE
www.sunsite.utk.edu/civil-war/warweb.html
A massive listing of Civil War web sites covering all aspects of the conflict.

LINCOLN HOME NATIONAL HISTORIC SITE
www.nps.gov/liho/index.htm
In addition to information about Lincoln's Springfield home, the site includes information on Lincoln's family, a Lincoln biography, Lincoln bibliography, a chronology of Lincoln's life, essays on Lincoln's life, and other writings about the 16th President.

LOOKING FOR LINCOLN
www.lookingforlincoln.com/
A heritage tourism project for the Central Illinois area which will eventually provide a more comprehensive look at Abraham Lincoln before he took his place in history. There are links to Lincoln sites in Illinois.

Travel Information

Kentucky

Elizabethtown Tourism and Convention Bureau, 1030 North Mulberry Street, Elizabethtown, KY 42701; tel. 800-437-0092 or 270-765-2175. www.ltadd.org/etowntourism/

Harrodsburg/Mercer County Tourist Commission, 103 S. Main Street, P.O. Box 283, Harrodsburg, KY 40330; tel. 800-355-9192 or 859-734-2364. www.harrodsburgky.com/

LaRue County Chamber of Commerce, 58 Lincoln Square, P.O. Box 176, Hodgenville, KY 42748; tel. 270-358-3411. www.laruecountychamber.org/

Lexington Convention and Visitors Bureau, 301 E. Vine Street, Lexington, KY 40507-1513; tel. 800-845-3959 or 859-233-7299. www.visitlex.com/

Springfield-Washington County Chamber of Commerce, 112 Cross Main Street, Springfield, KY 40069; tel. 859-336-3810. www.ltadd.org/springfield

Kentucky Department of Travel, 500 Mero Street #2200, Frankfort, KY 40601; tel. 502-564-4930. www.kytourism.com/

Indiana

Spencer County Visitors Bureau, P.O. Box 202, Santa Claus, IN 47571; tel. 888-444-9252. www.legendaryplaces.org/

Indiana Tourism Development Division, Indiana Department of Commerce, One N. Capitol, Suite 700, Indianapolis, IN 46204-2288; tel. 888-ENJOY-IN. www.enjoyindiana.com/

Illinois

Greater Alton/Twin Rivers Convention and Visitors Bureau, 200 Piasa Street, Alton, IL 62202; tel. 800-258-6645 or 618-465-6676. www.altoncvb.org/

Abraham Lincoln Tourism Bureau of Logan County, 303 Kickapoo, Lincoln, IL 62656; tel. 217-732-8687. www.logancountytourism.org/

Beardstown Chamber of Commerce, 121 North State Street, Beardstown, Illinois 62618; tel. 217-323-3271. www.beardstown.org/

Bloomington-Normal Area Convention and Visitors Bureau, 210 S. East Street, Bloomington, IL 61702-1586; tel. 800-433-8226 or 309/829-1641. www.visitbn.org/

Charleston Area Chamber of Commerce, Visitor Information Center, 501 Jackson, Avenue, Charleston, IL 61920; tel. 217-348-0430 or 217-345-7041. www.charlestontourism.org/

Chicago Office of Tourism, Cultural Center, 4th Floor, 78 E. Washington, Street, Chicago, IL 60602; tel. 312-744-2390. www.cityofchicago.org/tourism/

Danville Area Convention and Visitors Bureau, 101 W. Main, #146, Danville, IL 61834; tel. 800-383-4386. www.danvillecvb.com/index.ace

Decatur Area Convention and Visitors Bureau, 202 E. North Street, Decatur, IL 62523; tel. 800-331-4479 or 217-423-7000. www.decaturcvb.com/

Dixon Chamber of Commerce, 101 W. Second Street, Dixon, IL 61021; tel. 815-284-3361. www.dixonil.com/visitors.htm

Stephenson County Convention & Visitors Bureau, 2047 AYP Road, Freeport, IL 61032; tel. 800-369-2955 or 815-233-1357. www.stephenson-county-il.org/index3.html

Galena/Jo Daviess County Convention and Visitors Bureau, 101 Bouthillier Street, Galena, IL 61036; tel. 800-747-9377 or 815-777-4390. www.galena.org/

Galesburg Area Convention and Visitors Bureau, 2163 E. Main Street, Galesburg, IL 61401; tel. 309-343-2485. www.visitgalesburg.com/

Metamora Village Clerk, 100 N. Davenport Street, Metamora, IL 61548; tel. 309-367-4780.

Ottawa Visitors Center, 100 W. Lafayette Street, Ottawa, IL 61350; tel. 888-OTTAWA-4 or 815-434-2737. www.visit-ottawa-il.com/

Petersburg Chamber of Commerce, 125 S. 7th Street, Petersburg, IL 62675; tel. 217-632-7363. www.petersburgil.com/

Blackhawk Waterways Convention & Visitors Bureau, 201 N. Franklin Avenue, Polo, IL 61064; tel. 800-678-2108 or 815-946-2274. www.blackhawkwaterwayscvb.org/

Quincy Convention and Visitors Bureau, 300 Civic Center Plaza, Suite 237, Quincy, IL 62301-4161; tel. 800-978-4748 or 217-223-1000. www.quincy-cvb.org/

Southernmost Illinois Tourism Bureau, P.O. Box 278, Ullin, IL 62992; tel. 800-248-4373. www.southernmostillinois.com/southernindex.htm

Springfield Convention and Visitors Bureau, 109 N. Seventh Street, Springfield, IL 62701; tel. 800-545-7300 or 217-789-2360. www.visit-springfieldillinois.com/

Vandalia Chamber of Commerce, 1408 N. Fifth Street, P.O. Box 238, Vandalia, IL 62471; tel. 618-283-2728. www.vandalia.net/

Illinois Department of Commerce and Community Affairs, Bureau of Tourism, P.O. Box 1220, Macomb, IL 61455; tel. 800-2CONNECT.

Index

F

G

H

I

J

K

L